'Til Death Do Us Part
How Couples Stay Together

'Til Death Do Us Part
How Couples Stay Together

Jeanette C. Lauer and Robert H. Lauer

The Haworth Press
New York • London

'Til Death Do Us Part: How Couples Stay Together is monographic supplement #1 to *Marriage & Family Review*, Volume 10, 1986. It is not supplied as part of the subscription to the journal, but is available from the publisher at an additional charge.

The Haworth Press, Inc., 12 West 32 Street, New York, NY 10001
EUROSPAN/Haworth, 3 Henrietta Street, London WC2E 8LU England

Library of Congress Cataloging-in-Publication Data

Lauer, Jeannette C.
    'Til death do us part.

    Includes bibliographies and index.
    1. Marriage—United States. 2. Family life surveys—United States. I. Lauer, Robert H.
II. Title.
HQ734.L3363   1986   306.8'1   86-19583
ISBN 0-86656-601-5

Dedication

To our students at United States International University, who have been of invaluable help and, as always, to Jon, Julie, and Jeff, who have added immeasurable richness to our journey.

About the Authors

Jeanette C. Lauer is Associate Professor and Robert H. Lauer is Dean of the School of Human Behavior at United States International University in San Diego, California. The authors have published extensively on a variety of topics. Between them, they have published ten previous books and over 200 articles and chapters in books. Their last book together was a study of sexuality and sex roles in American utopian communities. Their interest in long-term marriages stems in part from their own 32-year marriage.

CONTENTS

Preface

In his description of an ideal society, Sir Thomas More noted that the Utopians sternly punished premarital sex on the grounds that otherwise very few people would ever get married. For who would want to spend a whole life with someone else and put up "with all the inconveniences that that involves" if one could have sexual intercourse outside of marriage? Sir Thomas was neither the first nor the last person to have a jaundiced view of long-term relationships. The subjects of this book, however, have a different view. According to them, there are indeed some "inconveniences" to marriage. But there are gratifications that are possible in a long-term marriage that far outweigh any inconveniences.

Two factors particularly stimulated this study. First, we had the experience of seeing the marriages of friends and relatives around us break up. We shared their pain in many cases, and endured the additional pain of coping with the loss of a couple with whom we had shared many meaningful experiences. Second, in trying to understand why some marriages failed and others lasted we were struck by the fact that there have been extremely few studies of marriages that succeed. A lot of information is available on why people break up, but next to nothing has been done on why people stay together.

As it turns out, people sometimes stay together in spite of the fact that they are unhappy with the marriage. We discuss the reasons for the stability of such unions in chapter 3. In other chapters, we show the factors that are operative in long-term, satisfying marriages, frequently comparing the results with the long-term but unhappy relationships. We also draw out the implications in the form of "action guidelines" for those who wish to apply the principles of our happily-married couples to their own relationships.

We are grateful to all the couples who participated in the research and willingly shared the details of their relationships. Their insights have enriched our own marriage. Hopefully, they will prove to be of help to many others for whom Utopia is not, as Sir Thomas would have it, a place where marriage is an inconvenience to be endured for the sake of sex, but a shared task to be engaged in for mutual fulfillment.

Jeanette C. Lauer
Robert H. Lauer

ix

'Til Death Do Us Part
How Couples Stay Together

Chapter 1
Three Couples:
Happily Ever After?

Who would you want to be if you had to be someone other than yourself? One man who was asked the question replied that he would like to be his wife's second husband. He obviously found his marriage to be extremely satisfying. Undoubtedly the more than four million Americans who are married each year would like to participate in the same kind of rich relationship enjoyed by the man and his wife. It is the kind of relationship that is heralded by countless stories and movies where the people lived happily ever after.

But "happily ever after" is a fairy tale ending. Or is it? To what extent do the realities of life square with the delicious fulfillment enjoyed by the fictional characters with whom we all became intimately acquainted in childhood? Most people, by the time they are adults, do not really expect to find the Prince Charming or the Cinderella who will insure them a life of bliss. Still, there is something hauntingly evocative about the notion of happily ever after. Most people, therefore, enter marriage with some hope of a long and satisfying relationship, a shared journey into an unknown but exciting future. Certainly, the three couples that we shall discuss in this chapter all entered their marriages with such hope. The couples are all real, but we have changed their names and some minor details to protect their identities. We will tell their stories as each of them told them to us.

JIM AND SANDRA

Jim and Sandra were married for four years when Sandra presented him with a unique anniversary present—her intention to get a divorce. Sandra's announcement left Jim stunned and perplexed. True, she had been in a bad mood for some weeks prior to the announcement. But she had always been somewhat moody, so

Jim had not been too concerned. When she proclaimed her intention to leave him, he suddenly realized that the "bad mood" was a symptom of some deeply-felt discontent, a discontent that he did not share and did not understand.

Jim and Sandra met in graduate school at a large university. Both came from stable homes. Both were excellent students. Both had decided to pursue business careers. They met at a reception for new students. There was no love at first sight, though Sandra caught his eye as "unquestionably the best looking woman in the group." He introduced himself to her and they began dating. Neither was committed to anyone else at the time.

According to their friends, and in their own thinking, Jim and Sandra were "made for each other." They understood each other because of the similarity of their backgrounds. They had been raised in the same kind of religious environment. They had the same kind of goals in life. They were interested in the same career. There were some differences, of course. Jim was interested—almost fanatically interested—in sports. Sandra enjoyed participating in some sports, but she did not share his desire to watch all kinds of sporting events on television. Sandra generally was more serious than Jim. Throughout his life, Jim had been a happy-go-lucky individual who was always sure that everything would turn out all right. He didn't worry about bills or tests or problems the way that Sandra did. But that was all right, they decided, because it meant that they were not only alike in many respects but also complemented each other well. Sandra would help Jim to be more responsible and Jim would help Sandra to relax a bit more and be less serious about various problems.

A few months after meeting, Jim and Sandra began living together. This experience only deepened their sense that they were truly compatible. They talked about marriage and about the kind of children that they would probably have. Their children would surely be beautiful, a combination of Sandra's cascading red hair and greenish eyes and Jim's infectious smile and gregarious nature. It was time to act. They invited their parents to meet each other and soon set the date for the wedding. They were to be married the year before graduation. Both sets of parents felt that it would be better to wait until after graduation, but Jim and Sandra looked upon their upcoming marriage as something that would add a dimension of adventure to their last year of school. Besides, their religious parents were not too happy with the idea of them living together without being married.

The wedding was a celebration. Sandra's parents spared no expense in providing a memorable affair. The happy couple rented an apartment near the university campus. They experienced few difficulties during that year in which they completed their degrees. After graduation, they located in another city, where both found jobs that they enjoyed. Their jobs were demanding, but challenging and rewarding. Mainly at Sandra's insistence, they saved a good deal of their income each month so that they could buy their own home. Three years after they were married, and two years after they had begun their careers, they moved into that home. It was modest, but it was theirs. "Happily ever after" seemed increasingly applicable to their lives.

In the next few months, however, Sandra became increasingly discontented. As far as Jim was concerned, everything seemed to be going well. He was not ecstatic, but he was content. His life had become more of a routine than an adventure, but that was acceptable. Sandra had never easily expressed her feelings to anyone, even to her own parents. She did not share her feelings with Jim during the months when her discontent was growing deeper and more intolerable. Ultimately, her unhappiness erupted into her statement that she wanted a divorce. He was stunned, and demanded an explanation. Finally, she began to tell him of some of the things that were irritating her. He was too messy, she said. He didn't pay enough attention to her. He was too willing to let her assume the responsibility for taking care of the home. He had let her down in almost every way. He did not fulfill her emotional, sexual, or social needs. She had come to the conclusion, she shouted at him, that there was no hope for their marriage and that divorce was the only thing that would satisfy her now.

Jim was startled. On reflection, he said, he knew that they were not as happy as they had been in the first year of their marriage. He realized that their life together had settled into something of a dull routine. Indeed, it was an irritating routine to Sandra. Still, he did not understand the intensity of her anger or her desire to leave him. "You don't get a divorce," he told us, "just because of minor annoyances." He felt that something else was going on with Sandra, but he had no idea what it could be. He never found out. The couple that was made for each other finalized the divorce a little over four years after their marriage. Jim remains perplexed about it all, some five years later. He has discovered that his experience was not unique, that many other couples he knew could not maintain their relationship beyond three to seven or eight years. He has begun to wonder if any marriage can last.

EDNA AND SAM

Edna and Sam could provide Jim with an answer. Yes, marriages do last. Their union has lasted for thirty years. Jim doesn't know Edna and Sam and, even if he did, he might not like their full answer. Edna and Sam live in a pleasant suburban home in the Midwest. They have one daughter, who has married and left the area. Sam is a blue-collar worker. Edna has worked at a variety of different jobs during their marriage, and now has a clerical position in a small business. Edna and Sam have a stable marriage; they agree that there is little probability that they will ever break up. But they also have an unhappy marriage. One could have almost said of them on the day that they married: "and they lived unhappily ever after."

Their unhappiness is not immediately evident to a casual acquaintance. They are pleasant, friendly people when they meet someone new, though they have few close friends. They do not bicker in public. But their marriage is a failure in terms of satisfying their needs for love and intimacy.

Edna's unhappiness, she admits, goes back farther in her life than her marriage. She was very unhappy in high school. She says that she never really liked herself when she was an adolescent. Unlike Jim and Sandra, she did not come from a stable, happy home. She grew up on a farm in her earliest years, then lived in a small town during her adolescence. She feels that she missed some of the pleasures of the growing-up years, because her mother worked and made Edna assume the responsibility for much of the housework. But the really painful memories of Edna do not involve the childhood experiences that were sacrificed to housework. The most painful memories are those of the relationships of her parents with each other and with her. Those memories still cause her to wince as she recalls them. She remembers virtually no expressions of love between her parents, and little expression of their love toward her. Her mother and father fought incessantly. They seemed to have little to talk about unless it was an argument of some kind. Sometimes, she recollects, her mother would disappear for the evening. On a number of those occasions, her father told Edna that her mother was out with other men.

Her father had difficulty expressing affection for Edna, but no difficulty in excercising discipline whenever he felt it necessary. He believed in corporal punishment. She remembers one time when he whipped her with his belt until it broke. Edna quit school when she was eighteen and got married. Her first marriage lasted only a short while. After the divorce, she moved to a different city and got a blue-collar job. There she met Sam. He was unmarried, good-looking, and, she soon discovered, fun to be with. She didn't love him, but he seemed to fall in love quickly with her. They got married within a few months. Sam wanted to get married because he was in love. Edna was willing to get married because she needed someone to care about her. Although Edna did not love Sam at the time, she was grateful to him for wanting her and for being willing to care for her. A little over a year after the marriage, their daughter, Judith, was born. Edna found herself not only feeling gratitude but a growing love for Sam.

The first two years of their marriage were among the happier times of Edna's life. She enjoyed having sex with Sam, more than she had ever enjoyed it with anyone else. She loved her daughter. She was financially secure, because Sam had a well-paying job. For a brief time, at least, it seemed that the trauma of her childhood had yielded to a normal, happy life.

Edna isn't sure when the erosion actually began. She was absorbed with the duties of motherhood. Sam began amusing himself by going out at night. They had sex less and less often. Finally, they never had it at all. Sam became more and more distant. When she complained, he simply said: ''I bring home the paycheck. You and Judy have plenty of food, a good house, and all the other stuff you need. Don't ask me for anything more.'' She knew that Sam was having affairs with other women, but she felt powerless to do anything about it. She was afraid to leave him, because she could not support herself and Judy. Furthermore, she didn't have any close friends and she could never return to her parents. ''Sam and Judy were all I had in the world,'' she told us. ''I didn't want to be alone again. So I settled for Sam as he is. We have a brother and sister relationship.''

When Judy got married and left the area, Edna and Sam had to face the fact that they had even less to bind them together. Edna felt the emptiness sharply. On occasion, she tried to rekindle something of their old relationship, but the chasm between them was apparently too wide to be bridged. Once, for example, she made a "pass" at him, and he rejected her. He told her bluntly that he simply had no sexual desire for her. She never tried again. They remain as brother and sister. At times, she admits, she feels disgust for him. But that passes, and she slumps back into a period of quiet despair over their relationship. She has come to terms with this. "Life is good now," she says, "compared to what it was with my first husband. One of the reasons I left him is that I got syphillis from him. He made me feel dirty." Life is also good now, she says, compared to what it was when she was a child. She has Judy, and hears from Judy and her son-in-law regularly. She has a job that she enjoys. She has a few friends with whom she socializes. Sam also has some friends with whom he goes out, mainly to a nearby tavern to drink and talk. Edna no longer desires sex with Sam. Sam no longer feels pressure from her to provide her with intimacy. The conflict, frustration, and hostility that marked most of their marriage is not as frequent or as intense as it used to be. They are not happy in their marriage, but at least they are not unbearably miserable. For the time being, that seems to be enough to keep them together.

Edna and Sam, then, raise another question. Can marriages not only last, but be happy as well? Jim and Sandra would not have wanted to duplicate the experience of Edna and Sam. Nor would most of us. The "ever after" is not very appealing without the "happily" appended to it.

LOUISE AND JEFF

Louise and Jeff have been married for over twenty years. They answer the question of whether marriage can be both long lasting and satisfying, and their answer is yes. Their marriage has not lasted because of a lack of problems or obstacles, however. In fact, they say that they have gone through a number of critical times and a number of rather dramatic changes in their lives.

The couple met in the Navy. Both had joined at about the same time. They were both officers. They married a few months after meeting. At first, the marriage tested them both. They had been independent, fairly self-sufficient individuals. They had each established a pattern of living that did not include a concern with the interests and wishes of another individual. They had to negotiate their married roles. Who would cook? Who would take care of which chores around the house? How much leisure time would they spend together and how much apart with former friends? How would they handle financial decisions, and who would take care of the finances?

In addition to searching for answers over the division of labor in the marriage, Louise and Jeff each had to adjust to being a part of a new, larger family. Jeff came from a small Swedish community in the Midwest; Louise was from Virginia. Because their courtship was so brief, neither had met most of the family of the other. Louise said that she had married not only Jeff, but a "whole community of Swedes." She had to learn to get along with a group of people who were delightful, but different from anyone she had known before.

Military families move a great deal. During the next five years, Jeff and Louise had two children and three different assignments. But they found life in the military to be exciting. Moving around the world did not bother them at this point. Jeff worked on his college degree, and Louise took care of the growing children as well as her own career in the Navy.

Their life together for the first seven years certainly seemed to demonstrate the possibility of "happily ever after." Then Jeff came home one day and announced that he would be going to Vietnam. That was a day Louise remembers with a shudder. The next few years, when Jeff was in Vietnam, were filled with anxiety for Louise. She felt that she had become very dependent on Jeff during the early years of their marriage, but when he shipped out to Vietnam, she said, "I again realized that I could manage alone." Yet these were years when their commitment to each other increased. War shatters the faithfulness of many couples, but Jeff and Louise were determined to maintain their love in spite of the difficult separation. When Jeff returned, they vigorously renewed their task of building a meaningful marriage and family life. Quickly, as Louise recalls, they succeeded in getting "on track" with each other and with their two children.

As it turned out, the couple survived the Vietnam War with greater ease than they did certain developments after the war. For a short time, everything was going well. "I don't know whether it was the war or the woman's movement," Louise said, "but I got restless. I wanted something more. I wasn't sure what. So I started to go to school myself." They continued to move around the country, of course, but Louise managed to finish her schooling. She eventually obtained a Master's degree in Counseling. Then came a time that she calls "our turbulent years." They were stationed in

California, and they seemed for the first time to start growing apart from each other. Louise was changing in a way that neither she nor Jeff had expected. The values and life-style that she had grown up with in Virginia seemed farther and farther removed from the things that she was hearing and reading and seeing in California. "I was changing so fast, that I was not sure what I believed," she told us. "My whole belief system had changed and I did not know what I believed." Jeff, however, remained fairly true to his Midwestern background. He did not understand some of Louise's new ideas about women and their role in the family and in society. Jeff was also changing in one way—he was wrestling with the idea of leaving the military. He now had his Master's degree—in business. California seemed to offer numerous opportunities for the ambitious, educated young man. Jeff began to dream of possibilities that could never be realized in the Navy.

Eventually, they decided to leave the military. Their children were now grown and away at college. Jeff went into business and Louise went back to school to get her Ph.D. She had a whole new future mapped out for herself as a female therapist who would be of special help to women. Had Jeff resisted her ambitions, their marriage may have run into more difficulty. Fortunately, though he was still puzzled somewhat by her feminist perspective, he decided that their relationship was more important to him than any disagreements they might have over such matters. The differences between them did not overshadow their continuing love. They had remained committed to each other even though their diverging perspectives were exerting strong tension on their relationship.

Eventually, they both modified their positions, coming closer together in the process. Louise felt that she had moved full-circle. She was independent before Jeff, then went through a phase when she felt very dependent on him. Now she was independent again, but that only meant that she was able to love her husband in a new and more meaningful way. Her love was no longer tangled up with dependence. She could live without him if necessary. But she didn't want to.

Similarly, while Jeff felt disquieted by her independence and her attitudes about men and women and their relationships, he did not berate her or try to change her. Rather, he tried to accept the "new" Louise, and found that this independent woman added a touch of excitement to their relationship. He began to see the woman's movement in a new light. Their "growing apart" years were over.

They are happier today than ever before. Their marriage has lasted, Louise told us, because they like each other as people, trust each other, and enjoy being together. Louise says that she would rather be with her husband than anyone she knows. Jeff, with a satisfied smile, acknowledges that he feels the same way about her.

THE PRECARIOUS JOURNEY

The three couples we have discussed illustrate the diversity of experiences that Americans find in marriage. Louise and Jeff probably represent the ideal of many Americans, as we shall discuss further in the next chapter. Perhaps most Americans get married with the perspective of Bill, a teacher who reflected back upon his wedding day of more than three decades ago:

> When I was married, I was in a kind of dream world. I didn't think there would be any problems in our marriage. Everything just seemed to be going right. We were starting off on what I thought would be a beautiful and exciting adventure together. I had always fantasized about meeting this beautiful young woman who would love me with the same intensity that I loved her, and with whom I would live in bliss through the rest of my life. On my wedding day, I thought that my fantasy had come true.

Bill's feelings on his wedding day are probably not too far removed from those of most Americans. But the journey upon which people embark when they are married is not the kind that Bill fantasized about. It is a precarious journey. For millions of Americans, the journey not only falls short of wedding-day fantasies, but also falls short of the experience of Louise and Jeff. Like Jim and Sandra, they wind up in divorce court. Or like Edna and Sam, they stick it out to the bitter end, grimly hanging on to a relationship that is satisfying to neither of them.

Young Americans who are aware of the precarious nature of the marital journey sometimes try to avoid the hazards by cohabitation. They live together for a period of time in order to see if they are compatible. About 2 million unmarried couples are now living together according to the U.S. Census Bureau. Not all of them even intend to raise the question of marriage. But among those that do, will they avoid the hazards of the journey? The evidence suggests that they will not.[1]

The arguments in favor of cohabitation as a preliminary step to marriage are reasonable enough. The couple can try out the relationship to see if it is truly meaningful to each of them. They can discover if they are sexually compatible. They can get a sense of the financial costs involved in maintaining a household. They can discover what each other is truly like and enter the marriage with more realistic expectations. They can determine the extent to which their individual life styles mesh together, whether they can find more fulfillment as a couple than as individuals.

In spite of the arguments, there are enough differences between cohabitation and marriage to make the former an inadequate preparation for the latter. The cohabiting couple can more easily break apart when problems between them arise. They normally construct their financial arrangements so that each has some financial independence, a situation that is uncommon in marriage. And the cohabiting couple doesn't have to make long-range plans. Finally, there is something about the commitment that goes into marriage that makes it a qualitatively different experience for most people.

The differences between marriage and cohabitation may not appear to be any stronger than the arguments in behalf of cohabiting, but researchers have found that cohabitation adds little if anything to the quality of marriage. Compared to those who have not, those who have cohabited are no more satisfied with their marriages, have no less conflict, have no greater closeness, and are not more likely to have an egalitarian marriage. In fact, one study even reported negative consequences from cohabitation. Alfred DeMaris and Gerald Leslie surveyed 309 recently married couples, about 71% of whom had cohabited.[2] They found that, compared to those who had not lived together before marriage, the cohabiters reported a lower degree of marital satisfaction. Furthermore, the women who had cohabited perceived the quality of commitment in their marriage as lower than did those who had not cohabited.

In spite of the stong arguments of the advocates, then, cohabitation does not appear to add anything to, and may even detract from, a satisfying marriage. The one exception to this is a study that reported that second marriages are likely to benefit from cohabitation.[3] According to the researchers, remarried couples who cohabited before marrying reported a more satisfying marriage than those remarried couples who had not cohabited.

If cohabitation is not the answer for first marriages, if it does not add to the probability of a long-term, satisfying relationship, what is the answer for those who desire such a relationship? What are the ingredients of a marriage that not only lasts but is rated as happy by both spouses? In an effort to address the question, we investigated people who have stayed together for 15 years or more. There are numerous works that tell us why people break up. But as one social scientist wrote over a decade ago, we still have not answered the question of ''what it is that makes marriages last, and enables them to survive.''[4] The conclusion is still valid. The works that tell couples how to construct a lasting and meaningful marriage tend to be based either upon the clinical experiences of those who have counseling troubled and dissolving marriages, or upon the speculations of those who believe that they have found the formula for success.

We did not try to find the ingredients of an enduring union by looking at broken marriages and asking what went wrong, but by examining marriages that have lasted and asking what was right. Of course, as Edna and Sam demonstrate, a marriage can last without being satisfying. In the course of the research, we found a number of couples who had less-than-satisfactory unions. We have included them in our analysis. In some cases, one of the partners is unhappy. We call these ''mixed marriages.'' In other cases, both partners are unhappy.

We shall describe our sample and procedures below. In the next chapter we will address the question of whether Americans truly want and realistically can have a long-term, happy marriage. In chapter three, we will discuss the various kinds of marriages that last, including both the happy and the unhappy kind. The remaining chapters will detail the ingredients of marriages that are both enduring and satisfying.

THE STUDY

There are 351 couples in our study. About one-fifth live in the Midwest, Texas and Georgia. The rest live in Southern California. We located them through our own friends and colleagues and through our students at United States International University in San

Diego. The only criterion for being included in the sample was being married a minimum of 15 years. We used 15 years for two reasons. First, it is slightly more than double the median number of years that those Americans who break up are married before the divorce or dissolution. It seemed reasonable, therefore, to say that 15 years is an enduring marriage. Second, the 15-year cutoff point allows us to include people who were married in the 1960s. Consequently, while some of the couples in our sample were married when divorce was a social stigma, others were married when divorce had become an acceptible option.

The couples gave us data in a number of ways. Most of them filled out a questionnaire, which included a question about the extent to which they were happy in their marriage.[5] Some of them wrote out for us an account of their relationship, identifying what they believed to be the factors in their enduring marriage. We also interviewed some of those who filled out questionnaires in order to supplement our information.

Although our original intent was to identify only those who had happy as well as enduring marriages, a number of couples with less than happy marriages responded to the questionnaire. This turned out to be a fortunate turn of events, for their responses gave us some interesting comparative information. In all, 300 of the couples indicated that both spouses were happy with their marriages. Thirty-two couples were "mixed," that is, one spouse was happy while the other was unhappy. And 19 couples were unhappy in their long-term marriages. The happy couples were married anywhere from 15 to 61 years, with a median marriage of 25.5 years. The mixed couples ranged from 15 to 47 years of marriage, with a median of 24.7 years, and the unhappy couples ranged from 15 to 43 years, with a median of 20.8 years.

Only 19 of the couples were childless. On the average, they had 2.6 children. Six-and-a-half percent of the couples were minorities—black, hispanic, or oriental. The remainder were white. Slightly over half (52.3 percent) had either a bachelor's degree or some graduate work. The majority had incomes in the $20 to $50,000 range. Thus, our sample is mainly middle to upper-middle class, though we had respondents from all social class levels (nearly 17 percent had 12 or less years of education, and 6.1 percent had annual family incomes under $20,000).

Finally, in terms of religious affiliation, 58.1 percent of the respondents were Protestant, 25.6 percent were Roman Catholic,

8.9 percent were Jewish, and 7.4 percent indicated no religious affiliation. The religious composition is fairly close to the national breakdown. A 1981 Gallup survey reported that 59% of Americans indicated Protestantism as their religious preference, 28% indicated Catholic, 2% said they were Jewish, and 7% said they had no religion. If our sample is any indication of national figures, we would have to say that Jewish couples are more likely than others to have a long-term marriage. Apart from that, Protestants, Catholics, and people with no religion appear in roughly the same proportion in our sample as they exist in the population as a whole. However, when we broke down religious affiliation by happy versus mixed versus unhappy couples, we found that a much higher proportion (13.2 percent) of the unhappy couples had no religious affiliation. Unhappiness in a long-term marriage can occur in all religious groups, but it may be particularly likely in a couple that has no religious affiliation.

We are prepared now to deal with the questions that form the basis for this study. What are the ingredients of a long-term marriage? What distinguishes happy from mixed and unhappy enduring marriages? As we shall see in subsequent chapters, there is no single factor, but a whole range of them.

FOOTNOTES

1. Much of the discussion on cohabitation is based on materials in Frank D. Cox, *Human Intimacy: Marriage, the Family and Its Meaning* (St. Paul: West Publishing Company, 1984), pp. 84–93.
2. Alfred DeMaris and Gerald R. Leslie, ''Cohabitation with the Future Spouse: Its Influence Upon Marital Satisfaction and Communication.'' *Journal of Marriage and the Family* 46 (February, 1984):77–84.
3. S. L. Hanna and P. K. Knaub, ''Cohabitation Before Marriage: Its Relationship to Family Strengths.'' *Alternative Lifestyles* 4 (1981):507–22.
4. J. H. Wallis, *Marriage Observed* (London: Routledge & Kegan Paul, 1970), p. 53.
5. The first thirty-two items on the questionnaire were the Dyadic Adjustment Scale. We added a number of statements with Likert-type responses relating to attitudes and feelings about the spouse and about marriage. We then asked each respondent to select the statements that best explained why he or she had remained married. Finally, we asked a number of open-ended questions about satisfaction over time, changes over time, and ways of dealing with problems and conflict.

Chapter 2
Is Marriage Obsolete?

Some years ago, the newspapers carried the story of a family that had built a fallout shelter in their yard. The husband, wife, and four children went into the shelter to live for awhile. Among other things, the husband said, "this will give us a chance to know each other better." A week later, the wife emerged from the shelter and left home with the youngest child. A few weeks after that, she filed a divorce suit, charging her husband with cruel and inhuman treatment. Apparently getting to know each other better did not enhance the quality of their lives.

This incident raises the question that we posed in the last chapter. Is a long-term marriage either desirable or practical? Do most Americans want such a marriage? And even if they do, does it make any difference? Can two people have a close and meaningful relationship over an extended period of time? Or have we reached a point in the modern world where, inside or outside of a fallout shelter, we will have to accept the fact that the old ideal of lifetime marriage that makes us happy ever after is simply not a viable option?

Both professional and lay people have argued that we are entering an era when an enduring marriage will increasingly not be an option. For instance, Herbert Otto has predicted that the ideal of the future "will not be marriage, children, and a house in the suburbs, but rather the experiencing of a series of deep and fulfilling relationships in a variety of environments."[1] Others have also prophesied the end of traditional marriage. Some have even argued not only that traditional family life in the nation is doomed, but that it *should* be doomed because it no longer in fits well with the nature of our society. America is changing rapidly. People are on the move. People are living longer on the average. It is increasingly difficult to maintain any kind of long-term relationship. And, some insist, it is in any case impossible to maintain an exciting and fulfilling relationship with one spouse over an extended period of time. As one young woman told us, "No one can have an exciting sex life with the same person for more than five years or so." Since

Americans have come to expect sexual fulfillment in their lives, the prospects for a long-term, happy marriage appear grim at best. At least, they are grim if we accept the foregoing arguments. Is, then, marriage doomed? Is it obsolete? Let us first look at the evidence for the prophecies of doom, namely, the precarious nature of marriages in America today. Then we will look at evidence on the other side of the picture.

THE CRUMBLING FOUNDATION

Traditionally, marriage and the family have been viewed as the bulwark of society. In 1966, a group of Catholic, Protestant, and Jewish organizations issued a statement about the family that reflects this traditional viewpoint. Among other things, the groups affirmed:

> We believe that the family is the cornerstone of our society. It shapes the attitudes, the hopes, the ambitions, the values of every citizen. The child is usually damaged when family living collapses. When this happens on a massive scale, the community itself is crippled.[2]

If the family begins to crumble, according to this view, then the foundation of our society crumbles as well.

There is a good deal of evidence that the foundation is indeed crumbling. More than a million couples a year now get divorced. Some social scientists predict that by the end of this century half of all marriages will end in divorce. The consequences of divorce are, of course, well known. For the husband and wife, in addition to economic costs, there is emotional trauma. For some people, divorce is a relief from an intolerable and destructive situation. Typically, however, those who divorce go through a process of grief that is akin to that endured by those who suffer loss through death. If there are children, they may become pawns in the struggle between the father and the mother. There have been some cases in recent years where one of the parents agreed to let the other take the children only in return for a substantial payment of money. There have been other cases where neither parent wanted the children. Children are probably better off in a broken, happy home than in an unbroken, unhappy home. But the pain of their parents separating is invariably intense. Children are typically upset initially, then go

through a period of anger and resentment. Eventu   18
adjust if they are given a happy home, and if there is
tension over relationships with their divorced parent.
    With over two million adults and more than one m\
involved in divorces each year, there is an enormou
trauma in American family life. But divorce is not the o   ....em
that plagues family life. Research on family violence has uncovered
a startling portrait that, at best, underestimates considerably the
amount of violence in American families. In one study of a
representative sample of the population, the researchers reported
that 16 percent of American couples admitted (we don't know how
many simply did not admit to their behavior) that they engaged in at
least one violent act against their spouse during the preceding year.[3]
At least 4 million Americans, both men and women, are abused to
some extent by a spouse during any one year. In addition, the
children are abused by their parents. Estimates of the extent of child
abuse vary widely, because mandatory reporting did not exist until
recent times. Estimates in the various pieces of research range from
tens of thousands to over a million children who are vulnerable to
physical injury each year.[4] It is hard to even estimate the amount of
psychological abuse that occurs in families every year, but it must
be added to the sordid list of family ills in America. When one looks
at this portrait of violence and dissolution, it is little wonder that
Better Homes and Gardens magazine found that 80 percent of the
more than 200,000 readers who responded to their poll agreed that
family life in America is in trouble.[5]

    Other things are happening to the American family which are not
violent, but indicative of serious changes and possible disruption.
That is, there are certain trends that underscore the fact that the
American family is changing, trends that are used by those who
prophesy the end of conventional marriage and family patterns. We
are not using "conventional" here in a negative sense. It does not
refer to the dreary repetition of the usual, but to the long-term
marriage in which there are children and a meaningful family life.
What, then, are the trends that seem to indicate that Americans are
searching for alternatives to the conventional? Consider the
following:

    —Between 1970 and 1983, the proportion of young women in
      the 20 to 24 age bracket that had never been married increased
      from 36% to 56%.

—Between 1970 and 1983, the number of couples cohabiting more than tripled.

—If current divorce rates continue, as many as half of all children will live in a fatherless family for a period of time before they are grown up.

—More than half of all married women have a job outside the home, and about half of all married women with preschool children in the home have jobs.

—Nearly one of every five babies born are to unmarried women.

—According to one national survey, 12% of all the children that women have borne were unwanted.

—There are over 1.5 million abortions each year.[6]

Such statistics suggest that increasing numbers of Americans no longer desire to have long-term marriages or a traditional family experience. At the least, they force us to ask the question, what do Americans really want in the way of marriage and family life?

Before answering the question of what Americans really want, we need to pause to put the current trends in perspective. This is not the first time in our history that people have seemed to turn away from conventional arrangements. Throughout our history, indeed even before we became a nation, there have been groups of people who have set up alternative communities in which there were economic, political, religious, educational, and marital arrangements that differed from those of the majority of Americans.[7] These communal groups, or communes as they are called today, have offered Americans a variety of different forms of marital and family life. Some were conventional in their marital and familial arrangements, but practiced a communistic form of economy. Others were unconventional in every way, ranging from the celibate groups to those that advocated a ''let everyone do their own thing'' philosophy to those that set up a group marriage. In the latter, everyone is married to everyone else. Couples-type relationships are discouraged or even forbidden. For no one is supposed to have exclusive access to anyone else. The entire group forms one family.

Thus, there have always been some Americans who searched for alternatives to a conventional marriage and family life. But the numbers of people involved in the trends noted above suggest that the proportion of those involved in the search has risen dramatically. Or has it? What exactly do the trends signify? What do Americans really want?

WHAT DO WE WANT?

Do the present trends reflect new ideals? Or are they the painful outcome of a people who have found their ideals trampled in the dust of rapid change? We believe that the answer to both questions is, in part, yes. That is, there are some new ideals, but those new ideals are not radically different from the past. Not all of the trends noted above represent what Americans *prefer*. In some cases, at least, they represent what Americans have done in an effort to adjust to a changing world. In particular, we do not believe that most Americans prefer alternative forms of marriage and family life. What are the alternatives? In addition to cohabitation, which we discussed in the last chapter, and the various options such as group marriage that have been offered by the communal groups, there is the alternative of what has been called "progressive" or "serial" monogamy, which is having a series of spouses, one at a time, but without the stigma or problems of divorce proceedings. Those who advocate this system affirm the importance of marriage, but say that we should make divorce easier rather than more difficult. Marriage, in other words, is very important, but long-term marriages are not. Others have suggested a second alternative—the trial marriage, which could be for a specified period of time with the possibility of renewing the contract for an additional time period. Again, advocates of trial marriage affirm the importance of marriage, but see no particular virtue in making marriage a long-term commitment. The open marriage has also been touted as an attractive alternative. In the open marriage, partners decide where each will have the right to sexual and companionate relationships with someone other than the spouse.

There are still other alternatives, such as the single life with a series of sexual partners. But while some of these alternatives may be titillating as people fantasize about them, they are not generally viewed as realistic or even desirable options. Consider the following facts.[8] Of the more than 50 million Americans who are single, only a minority are single by choice. Three-fourths of a national sample of high school seniors reported that having a good marriage and family life would be "extremely important" to them. More than 90 percent of American youth indicate that they expect to be married, and most of them are optimistic about the chances for a long-term marriage. The great majority of adults who have been surveyed also say that a good marriage and family life is one of the most important factors in their happiness. In terms of actual practice, Americans continue to marry in record numbers. Furthermore, most of them say that they are satisfied with their marriages and their family life. In one national survey, 78 percent of adults reported a "great deal" of satisfaction with family life, while only 3 percent said they got little or no satisfaction from it. Two-thirds of those adults also said they were "very happy" with their marriages, while only 3 percent indicated that they were "not too happy." In the *Better Homes and Gardens* survey noted above, 81 percent of the respondents said they would marry their present spouse if they had a chance to do it over again. Finally, a Gallup survey reported that 92 percent of Americans would welcome a greater emphasis on "traditional family ties."

In other words, there appears to be a renewed and strong interest in marriage and family life. Most people do not find the alternatives attractive. They are not enamored of the single life nor of any of the alternative forms of marriage and the family. There is one difference from the past, however. Americans do not necessarily want the traditional marriage in which the husband is the breadwinner while the wife remains at home to care for the house and children. Some Americans still idealize the traditional arrangement, but increasing numbers prefer a marriage in which the woman has more options and the couple share a greater number of household tasks. That is why we said above that there are both some new and some old ideals that are operating. Americans have not cast out monogamous marriage and the nuclear family, but they are turning away from the traditional format of dominant husband and submissive, stay-at-home wife.

Is what we want practical? The statistics on divorce and cohabitation suggest that it may not be. But those statistics reflect, we believe, a transitional time in American life. We have been grappling with the sexual revolution and we have been struggling with the problem of working out an arrangement that is fairer to women. Furthermore, it is no longer a stigma to be divorced nor is there a great deal of pressure on young people to get married and have children. At one time, a stable marriage was virtually a necessity for an aspiring young corporate executive. Parents and in-laws and other relatives might put considerable pressure on a young couple to have children. But now it is acceptable to be single or to be married and childless.

Americans are seeking to come to terms with the sexual revolution, the woman's movement, and the greater freedom to choose one's marital status and lifestyle. Many of those who plunged into the revolution and the movement and the new freedom with zest have emerged with a sense of emptiness, a hunger unsatisfied, a quest that ended in a thicket of disillusionment. For they believed that they had to discard the ideal of long-term marriage in order to reach the new heights of meaningfulness. Now, increasing numbers of Americans are wistfully looking toward the possibility of a stable marriage again. Swinging has not brought sexual fulfillment. The single life has not fulfilled its promise of endless adventure. The childless life has lost some of the glamour that made it appealing to many women in the 1960s and 1970s. It is not a recapturing of the past in which we are now engaged. Rather, it is a recognition that we threw away too much. It wasn't necessary to reject stable marriages in order to affirm sexual fulfillment and sexual equality and freedom of choice. Increasing numbers of Americans are aware of that fact, and are struggling now to wed fulfillment and equality with a stable relationship. Maritable stability is not only what Americans prefer, it is also what Americans need. For in a number of fundamental ways, a stable marriage is good for us. We do not always prefer that which is best for us. But in this case, the ideal also happens to be that which enhances our well-being, a point we shall discuss next.

THE BENEFITS OF AN ENDURING MARRIAGE

Many Americans have been raised on the notion that whatever is good for us has to taste bad or be painful, and that, as a result, we seldom desire those things that are good for us. Whatever the validity of that notion, Americans' preference for an enduring marriage contradicts it. In this case, people desire something that has numerous benefits.

Intimacy

Consider first of all our need for intimacy. Social psychologists point out that we all have a basic need to establish intimate relationships. "There is a universal and primitive longing to be attached, to relate, to belong, to be needed, and to care."[9] We only find fulfillment as we engage in meaningful relationships with others.

We do, of course, have intimate relationships with friends and relatives. But marriage offers us a unique kind of intimacy, an intimacy that can be our emotional salvation in an impersonal, competitive world. As anyone who observes people in a metropolitan area knows, there are a lot of lonely people in America. And when we are isolated or lonely, we are something less than complete humans. John Steinbeck once wrote that during a period of eight months when he lived alone in the mountains, he realized that he had stopped whistling, stopped talking to his dogs, and stopped having feelings other than simple pain and pleasure. We can only enjoy the full range of human emotions, he said, through our relationships with others.

Isolation from others is dehumanizing. Loneliness is destructive. Lonely people have more problems of physical and emotional health than people who are not lonely. Lonely people do not think as highly of themselves as those who are not lonely. And lonely people tend to die at an earlier age than those who are not lonely. It is no exaggeration to speak of our *need*, and not merely our *desire*, for intimacy.

How do we establish intimate relationships? As a result of the sexual revolution, the high rate of marital breakup, and the mobility of Americans, a whole range of new mechanisms have appeared for bringing people together. Singles housing complexes, singles bars, singles parties, and singles clubs are available in cities. Some people advertise—"white male, mid-40s, college graduate, wide range of interests, seeks interesting companion in her 30s or early 40s." Others pay a fee to a dating service. The old standbys are still used, of course—friends get you a date or you meet someone through church. But the new mechanisms are flourishing. They bear mute testimony to our craving for intimacy.

Some Americans have set out on the quest for intimacy through brief, even casual, relationships. Men who go to singles bars are frequently looking for a "one-night stand" or a temporary "no strings attached" relationship. The quest is self-defeating. Intimacy demands commitment. To refuse to commit yourself to another is to refuse to love the other. And the refusal to love is the abdication of intimacy. The casual relationship not only diverts us from attaining intimacy, but also intensifies our loneliness. As psychoanalyst Erich Fromm wrote, a focus on sexual orgasm, rather than on the relationship with the other person, can be like alcoholism and drug addiction: "It becomes a desperate attempt to escape the anxiety engendered by separateness, and it results in an ever-increasing sense of separateness, since the sexual act without love never bridges the gap between two human beings, except momentarily."[10]

Many Americans have discovered through grim experience the futility of trying to satisfy intimacy needs through casual relationships. Joseph, a strikingly handsome acquaintance of ours, was known to his office coworkers as an inveterate flirt and a man on the prowl. He had a wife and young child at home, but many of the young women with whom he worked were captivated by his charm. He had a full schedule of lunches and meetings with them in various places. It was no surprise to anyone who knew Joseph when he announced that he was getting a divorce. The divorce was his wish, of course, and not his wife's. When Joseph was "free," he eagerly pursued the life of the swinging single. During those days, we once asked him how he was enjoying it. We expected to hear a long tale of triumphs and thrills. Instead, he said, with an obvious note of regret in his voice: "It's okay. But you know, I miss having a shared past with someone. I miss the continuity. It's like you have to keep starting all over, again and again." He paused, and no doubt noticed the look of surprise on our faces. "Oh, I'm enjoying it. But, you know, you don't have any of those experiences that make your relationship special because you shared them together and because no one else had them exactly like the two of you." Some months later, we received a wedding invitation from Joseph. He is now trying a second time to fulfill his needs through a stable marriage.

Uniquely shared experiences are part of the emotional balm provided by a stable marriage. They are a crucial part of the experience of intimacy. One couple in our sample divorced after over twenty years of marriage. They remarried after two years, and report that they are happier than ever now. During the time that they were divorced, the husband told us, he would think about all of their shared experiences and realize that the hardest part of the separation was the loss of continuity. "I knew that I wanted to be buried next to her," he said. "I knew that I didn't want to grow old without her with me. We had too much invested in each other, too many things that we had done together. It just killed me to think of going to our childrens' weddings or seeing grandchildren or working for retirement without her."

Of course, intimacy is also love and affection and caring. We shall answer the question of whether (and how) those qualities can be maintained with the same person over an extended period of time in chapter 5. Here, we shall simply quote from one of the women in our sample, Maria, who has been married for 15 years. Maria had both a deep need for, and a fear of, intimacy when she was married.

I was the second child in a family of four. My father has a personality problem. He is a heavy drinker. He spent long hours at work and always worried about our finances. There was constant fighting and bickering in the house. I saw my father drunk nightly as a child. I remember thinking that I didn't want to get married myself.

When I look back at my feelings as a child, I realize that I was neither loved nor accepted. We had an almost affectionless environment. There was no hugging and kissing between family members.

Hank and I met when we were both twenty five. After ten months we were married. We were attracted to each other in many different ways. Sexually, we are fortunate to be compatible. Because of the lack of affection during my childhood, I at first had problems accepting Hank's love. But after fifteen years, I have worked through that. I love Hank for his qualities. He is loyal and he has maintained intimacy with me. I have learned that I can depend upon him. We both talk about how fortunate we are to have a happy, successful marriage.

Happiness

"All men," wrote Pascal, "seek happiness. That is without exception. Whatever different means they employ, they all tend to this end."[11] Over two centuries later, Sigmund Freud agreed that humans all strive for happiness. In fact, he argued, we are by our very nature driven to find happiness. The pleasure principle dominates our mental processes from the beginning of life. But he noted gloomily that the pleasure principle "is at loggerheads with the whole world."[12] That is, we are necessarily driven to find something that of necessity will always elude us. For full happiness would require the free expression of our instincts, and those instincts are invariably suppressed by the social order. Society—no society—can allow people to run around freely behaving according to their own instinctual needs. We have to compromise with those needs in order to maintain an orderly society. We give up, therefore, a measure of happiness in order to achieve the stability and benefits of civilized society.

Freud notwithstanding, Americans have come to view personal happiness as that which is desirable and attainable and even a right. To some extent, stable marriages have been the victim of this pursuit of happiness. Why should I stay married if it means that I will stay unhappy? Or why should I stay married if I can find greater happiness with someone else? From this perspective, Edna and Sam, the unhappy couple we described in the last chapter, are foolish. It borders on the insanely ludicrous for a man and a woman to remain together for decades and torment each other with their mutual unhappiness.

We would not disagree with the foolishness of the situation of Edna and Sam. But neither would we agree that happiness is just waiting around the corner of the next spouse or of single life. An enduring marriage is not a cure-all. But a happy marriage is an integral part of a happy life. Several years ago, *Redbook* magazine published the results of an interesting survey of 52,000 of their readers on happiness. Who are the happiest women? Those who jauntily pursue the pleasures of the single life? Those who are enmeshed in the intricacies of a meaningful career? Those who are wholly involved in home and family? No, the "women who go off the charts in happiness are middle-aged, just past menopause, unburdened by their now-grown children; and—perhaps most important—they are women who all along have had access to satisfaction in *both* family life and outside work."[13] In other words, they are women who have achieved the ideal we noted above—a conventional, but nontraditional, marriage in which they can pursue fulfillment both as wives and mothers and as workers in the marketplace.

Two researchers at the University of Texas, using data from six national surveys of Americans, underscore the importance of marital happiness to a happy life.[14] They attempted to answer the question, what factors contribute most to general happiness? Looking at seven aspects of life, ranging from friendships to work to marriage, they found that marital happiness contributed more to general happiness than anything else.

This is not to say that one can't be single and happy, or that one can't find happiness through a succession of marriages. And, as Edna and Sam constantly remind us, it is possible to have a long-term marriage that only maintains one's misery. Nevertheless, the majority of Americans claim that marital happiness is the most important factor in their general happiness. And those in enduring and happy marriages can speak in moving terms about the contribution of their relationship with their spouses to their lives. Dick, a manager who has been married more than thirty years, told us:

I have thought from time to time about my own death. And I've wondered about my wife and children. How will they take it? I've been with enough friends who have had family members die to know that people often feel guilty. They feel that they didn't do enough for the person who died, or they didn't let the person know how much they really cared, or something like that. So I've fantisized about my death. Because one of the things I would want to do is call my family to my bedside and say to them: "Remember one thing. You must not feel guilty after I'm gone. Because you have made me one of the happiest men in the world. You have made life beautiful for me. Don't have any regrets. Just remember the love. Remember how grateful I am for each of you."

Physical and Mental Health

Surveys of Americans have shown that one of the most prominent personal concerns is health. The great majority of Americans rank health as one of the most important factors in the quality of their lives. Americans literally spend billions of dollars per year on products—including many that physicians say are worthless—that will improve or maintain their health.

Those who yearn for good health would do well to strive for a happy marriage. For, among other things, a happy marriage seems to contribute to both physical and mental health. There are long-standing jokes that poke fun at the idea: "Do the married live longer than single people? No, it just seems longer." But in spite of the jokes, the fact remains that a good marriage appears to buttress good health. Those who are happily married are likely to enjoy better physical health than those who are not married. Frances Kobrin and Gerry Hendershot looked at mortality rates in the United States to test the thesis that marriage and family contribute to people's longevity.[15] The researchers examined 20,000 deaths of people aged 35 to 84. They found that death rates were lower for married persons than nonmarried persons in all age brackets, lower for those with children than those without children, and lower for single people who were heads of households than for those who were not heads. The best explanation for such results, they argue, is that the ties of marriage and family somehow protect people, probably by providing them with the intimate relationships that are vital to their well-being. A good marriage also enhances our emotional well-being. As Rubenstein and Shaver point out in their book on loneliness, research has shown that married people are generally better off psychologically than are single people.[16] Among the roughly 30,000 people who responded to their questionnaire, the married reported being less lonely, happier, and healthier than the unmarried. Other researchers have found lower rates of depression and far less use of psychiatric help among the happily married.

But, as one of our respondents noted, there may be an ironic twist to an enduring and happy marriage. "I have a feeling," he said, "that it will be devastating if she dies before I do. But I guess that will have to be the cost of all the years of fulfillment." Do those who have a happy marriage that contributes to their health and well-being pay a price in the end of emotional devastation? Interestingly enough, the answer is no. Colin Parkes and Robert Weiss interviewed a number of widows and widowers, scheduling an initial and a follow-up interview with most of them.[17] They sought to identify the factors involved in "good" versus "poor" outcomes of the grief process. Why did some people seem to sink into a pathological grief pattern, while others seemed to bear up well under their grief and to come to terms with their loss? The intensity and duration of mourning, the researchers noted, should be related to the quality of the marriage that was lost. And their data supported that expectation, but in a "paradoxical" way:

> It seems not to have been the good marriages, that marriages in which there was contentment and mutual acceptance, where misunderstandings were infrequent, whose end was following by unending grief. On the contrary, difficulties in recovery seemed more frequently to occur following the loss of marriages which were conflict-ridden, thoroughly troubled, in which one or the other spouse may well have contemplated separation and divorce.[18]

The researchers found that those with poor marriages did not seem as afflicted by the loss at first as those with good marriages.

They appeared less overwhelmed and more able to participate in activities with others. But as time wore on, they increasingly appeared jammed into a grieving pattern, unable to accept the loss and engaged in reproaching themselves and longing for the return of the dead spouse. Parkes and Weiss suggest that this continuing grief on the part of those who had unhappy marriages may be, in part, a kind of penance ("I will atone for my lack of love while my spouse lived by continuing to grieve"), and, in part, grief over the good marriage that never existed. They quote one woman who said that she kept thinking that if her marriage had been happier, her husband may not have contracted the cancer that killed him. By contrast, a woman who had a good marriage said, some thirteen months after the death of her husband, that the memory of their happiness made her feel good. She believed that she would have felt worse had their marriage been less happy—she would have kept thinking of what she should have done to make it better. As it was, she felt good because the marriage was good.

THE FUTURE OF MARRIAGE

The future of marriage looks different to us than it does to the prophets of family doom. We do not accept the notion that conventional marriage and family life is inevitably dying out in our nation. As noted above, surveys show that Americans clearly prefer a stable, monogamous marriage and a stable family life over any of the alternatives that have been suggested and tried. But preferring something doesn't mean that we can have it. If a new trend of stability is to be attained, Americans will have to learn how to deal with the meaning of sexual fulfillment, with equality between men and women in the maritial relationship, with women's right to pursue a career, with an equitable division of labor in the home, and with the necessity of commitment that is freely chosen when social pressures to commitment are weak.

The years ahead are going to be years of learning. Americans desire, and essentially feel that they have a right to, such things as sexual fulfillment and happiness in their relationships. Americans are solidly pursuing the quest for personal fulfillment. An enduring marriage can be an important element in that fulfillment, but such marriages, even though they still represent the idea, seem to be attained by a steadily diminishing number of people. That trend, we believe, will be reversed as Americans learn how to maintain an enduring and rewarding relationship while dealing with such problems as sexual equality and coming to terms with new factors on the scene such as the romanticization of singlehood. The learning process, furthermore, can be facilitated by a close examination of those who are realizing the ideal. What are the critical factors that make the difference between couples like Jim and Sandra, Edna and Sam, and Louise and Jeff? How do some people manage to stay together while couples all around them are splitting up? How do some not only manage to stay together but apparently revel in their relationship while others only stay together and grimly live it out? In the next chapter, we will look at the various types of enduring marriages, including those that are basically unsatisfying. Following that, we will examine the ways in which the happily married couples in our sample manage to construct a long-term, fulfilling marriage, including the ways in which they differ from those who are long-term but unhappily married.

FOOTNOTES

1. Herbert A. Otto, "Man-Woman Relationships in the Society of the Future," *The Futurist*, April, 1973, p. 60.
2. *American Families: Trends and Pressures, 1973*. Hearings before the Subcommittee on Children and Youth of the Committee on Labor and Public Welfare, United States Senate, September 24, 25, and 26, 1973 (Washington, D.C.: Government Printing Office, 1974), p. 278.
3. R. J. Gelles and M. A. Straus, "Violence in the American Family," *Journal of Social Issues* 35 (no. 2):15–39.
4. Marian Eskin, *Child Abuse and Neglect* (Washington, D.C.: U.S. Department of Justice, 1980).
5. Kate Keating, "What's Happening to American Families?" *Better Homes and Gardens*, July, 1983, pp. 24–36.
6. The figures are from: Arland Thornton and Deborah Freedman, "The Changing American Family," *Population Bulletin* 38 (October, 1983) and the *Statistical Abstract of the United States, 1982–83*.
7. The sexual arrangements of the various groups are detailed in Robert H. Lauer and Jeanette C. Lauer, *The Spirit and the Flesh: Sex in Utopian Communities* (Metuchen, N.J.: The Scarecrow Press, Inc., 1983).
8. See: *Psychology Today*, August, 1983, p. 78; "Marriage vs. Single Life," *IRS Newsletter*, Autumn, 1982, p. 8; Thornton and Freedman, "The Changing American Family," p. 6; Andrew Cherlin and Frank F. Furstenberg, Jr., "The American Family in the Year 2000," *The Futurist*, June, 1983, p. 7; and the *Gallup Report*, no. 197, February, 1982.
9. F. Phillip Rice, *Contemporary Marriage* (Boston: Allyn & Bacon, 1983), p. 6.
10. Erich Fromm, *The Art of Loving* (New York: Bantam Books, 1956), p. 10.
11. Blaise Pascal, *Pensees* (New York: The Modern Library, 1941), p. 134.

12. Sigmund Freud, *Civilization and Its Discontents*, trans. James Strachey (New York: W. W. Norton, 1961), p. 22.

13. Gail Sheehy, "The Happiness Report," *Redbook*, July, 1979, pp. 54–59.

14. Norval D. Glenn and Charles N. Weaver, "The Contribution of Marital Happiness to Global Happiness," *Journal of Marriage and the Family* 43 (February, 1981):161–68.

15. Frances E. Kobrin and Gerry E. Hendershot, "Do Family Ties Reduce Mortality? Evidence From the United States, 1966–1968," *Journal of Marriage and the Family* 39 (November, 1977):737–45.

16. Carin Rubenstein and Phillip Shaver, *In Search of Intimacy* (New York: Delacorte Press, 1982), pp. 90–91.

17. Colin Murray Parkes and Robert S. Weiss, *Recovery From Bereavement* (New York: Basic Books, 1983).

18. *Ibid.*, pp. 97–98.

Chapter 3
Enduring Is Not Enough

In the past, a marriage was judged to be successful if it lasted and produced children. Today, Americans expect something more from their marriage. They want to be fulfilled. They want happiness. When we first discussed this research with others, an acquaintance illustrated for us this belief in the right to happiness. We had spoken of our interest in pursuing the reasons why some people have enduring marriages. He responded negatively to the phrase "enduring marriage." "I don't like it," he said. "The word 'enduring' bothers me. You make it sound like marriage is a matter of endurance, of somehow gritting your teeth and lasting it out. I wouldn't want to stay in that kind of marriage." Like Americans generally, he believed in the right to happiness and in the role of marriage in creating that happiness.

Because of this emphasis on happiness and fulfillment through marriage, we had assumed that most people today would not tolerate an unsatisfying union over an extended period of time. As our research quickly showed, and as discussions with marriage and family therapists confirmed, some people stay together in spite of the prevalence of divorce and in spite of their personal dissatisfaction with their relationship.

Indeed, "dissatisfaction" is too mild a word for some relationships. It is not just that some people are willing to accept and live with a marital relationship that is tolerable though unfulfilling. There are those who remain in a marriage that is destructive to their well-being. A woman wrote to columnist Ann Landers about the relief and joy she felt when her husband died. She stayed in the marriage for only one reason, she said—she needed the financial support of her husband in order to raise their children. After 40 years of marriage, her alcoholic husband died and she was "free at last." The woman said that there were countless others just like her, who actually rejoice in, rather than mourn, the death of a spouse, who find widowhood a release from misery rather than confinement into loneliness.

Was this woman an exception to the tendency for those in unhappy marriages to have a more difficult adjustment to the death of a spouse? Is she right that many women are "closet widows" who greet a husband's death with relief rather than grief? She may be an exception, but her letter seethed with bitterness and anger. The point is, her letter underscores the intensity of the unhappiness of some people's long-term marriages.

Our primary interest is the enduring and satisfying marriage, the union that not only lasts but is fulfilling to each of the spouses. And, as we showed in the last chapter, such a marriage is still the ideal of most Americans. If that ideal is to be achieved, it is important to recognize the ways in which only the enduring part is achieved. That is, it is important to be aware of the traps into which people fall in their quest for a satisfying as well as a long-term union. The traps are various kinds of relationships which are stable, but not fulfilling. There are, of course, some marriages that remain together because the two people fulfill the neurotic needs of each other. As comics like to point out, the union of a masochist and sadist fulfills the needs of each. At a more realistic level, there are numerous matchups that illustrate the way in which people fulfill each other's neurotic needs, such as the union of the man who needs to be mothered with the woman who needs to mother someone. Such unions may be stable, but we do not regard them as truly fulfilling. They satisfy neurotic needs, but they do not result in the individuals becoming what Carl Rogers called fully-functioning people.

In addition to the neurotic union, there are various other kinds of marriages that are long-term. John Cuber and Peggy Harroff have identified five kinds of long-term marriages that range from the fulfilling to the turmoil-laden.[1] Three of their types illustrate the trap of an enduring but unfulfilling marriage: the conflict-habituated, the devitalized, and the passive-congenial. Two of their types illustrate the enduring and endearing union that is the American ideal: the vital marriage and the total marriage.

THE CONFLICT-HABITUATED MARRIAGE

This marriage is characterized by more or less continual conflict and tension. At its worst, the two spouses engage in private quarreling and nagging each other, but their differences do not remain private. Friends and relatives become aware of their disagreements because they tend to bring up the faults and deficiencies of each other in public. At its best, the two spouses generally maintain a fairly harmonious public front, "but after a few drinks at the cocktail party the verbal barbs begin to fly."[2] The spouses recognize that they are largely incompatible, and that they live under more-or-less continual tension. They stumble together along the precarious edge of the precipice of destructive conflict.

Cuber and Harroff illustrated the conflict-habituated marriage with the account of a physician who was married for twenty-five years to a woman he had known since high school. He pointed out that even then they had quarreled. Their relationship had been a long, running battle. They disagreed over virtually everything except the welfare of their children. The only reason they married, he opined, was that they had had such good sexual relations together. He thought it strange, on reflection, that he and his wife had such a marriage. He would not, he asserted, tolerate such conflict in any other relationships. But he did, and always had, acquiesced to it with his wife.

As we shall point out in chapter 7, conflict per se is not destructive. In fact, the absence of conflict may be a danger sign in a marriage. Happy couples strike a medium between total absence and pervasive presence of conflict in the relationship. Conflict and good conflict-management skills enhance the quality of marriage. Habitual conflict makes the marriage an endurance contest rather than an adventure in fulfillment.

THE DEVITALIZED MARRIAGE

A devitalized marriage is one that begins with an intense sense of being in love and of enjoying and indentifying with each other. The couple in a devitalized marriage perceive the early days of their union as one of deep love, shared times, satisfying sexual relations, and a sense of belonging to each other. But over time, the relationship gradually erodes into dull experiences and ritualized behavior. They no longer spend much time together. They do not have an exciting sex life. They take adequate care of family responsibilities, but they do not share many interests and activities.

There are two subtypes of the devitalized marriage. In one, the couple go through the rituals of family life, including such things as attending functions involving the children. But the spouses are like two separate entities who just happen to be engaged in the same task at the same time. They take each other for granted. They are not fully involved in each other as persons. They do not enter into each other's experiences at a deep level. They simply intersect at the point of overt behavior.

The second subtype differs in that one of the spouses refuses to mutely accept the situation. The rebellious spouse continues to engage in the rituals, but resists the idea that the situation is acceptable. The rebellious spouse longs for the excitement of the early days of the marriage, but may not know quite how to go about restoring any of that excitement. Thus, one spouse is content to let the ritualization continue, while the other is bristling with a desire to change.

In either case, the devitalized marriage will probably continue. There is no serious conflict to force the couple to confront the void in their relationship. The rituals of family life, particularly where there are children, may be sufficiently consuming of energy that little thought is given to alternatives. There may be family or religious pressures to keep the marriage intact. The net result is that the relationship plods on.

Cuber and Harroff pointed out that the devitalized marriage is "exceedingly common." The participants may justify remaining together by comparing themselves with other couples who appear to have the same kind of relationship. They may give the rationale that their experience is what people must expect in any long-term relationship, that all marriages necessarily become like theirs. They may also insist that they do continue to share some things that are meaningful and important, even if that is nothing more than the memory of more vibrant times. The important point is that those in a devitalized marriage may not define themselves as deprived. One of the reasons they may stay together is that, while they recognize the loss of vitality in their relationship, they define the loss as normal.

THE PASSIVE-CONGENIAL MARRIAGE

The passive-congenial marriage is quite similar to the devital-ized, "the essential difference being that the passivity which pervades the association has been there from the start."[3] That is, the dullness and ritualization were present from the very beginning.

This marriage never had an exciting beginning. There is no deterioration of vitality because the relationship began on a low plane and stayed there. There is not likely to be much conflict in this marriage. The spouses tend to be comfortable with each other and to share at least some interests and activities. The decision to get married may have been primarily rational rather than emotional, a weighing of the advantages and disadvantages of this particular mate.

Cuber and Harroff identified two different ways that people may come into a passive-congenial marriage. One is that they simply drift into it. They somehow meet, date, and eventually drift into marriage, perhaps because friends or family expect the marriage to take place. They did not care deeply for each other from the beginning. They get along well together, but never experience any intense feelings for each other. The marriage therefore is a continuation of a congenial though lackluster relationship.

The other way that people come into a passive-congenial marriage is by deliberate choice. The two individuals may be primarily interested in their careers. They may define marriage as desirable in some sense, but they do not want to make much emotional investment in a marital relationship. The workaholic, for example, may enter a passive-congenial union out of practical necessity (he or she has someone to care for the house, cook meals, do errands, etc.). In some careers, it is expedient to have a mate; the marriage becomes an acceptable way to fulfill one of the requirements for rapid career mobility.

In essence, then, the passive-congenial marriage allows the participants to pursue their real interests. The marriage may make few emotional or time demands on them. Unlike those in a devitalized relationship, they have no regrets over loss because they never expected anything more than they have. And in at least some cases, they actively prefer what they have.

THE VITAL MARRIAGE

In a vital marriage, the spouses do many of the same things as those in the above three. That is, they engage in many of the same kinds of family and community activities. But there is a significant difference, for those in a vital marriage have an emotional bond and a depth of sharing that is lacking in the three types of marriages discussed above. Their lives are inextricably woven together, so that there is an intensity of shared feelings and involvement in their activities. It is the presence of each other that gives special meaning to activities. Whereas those in a passive-congenial marriage find intrinsic pleasure in activities independently of the spouse, those in the vital marriage find pleasure in the *shared* experience. Those in a vital marriage prefer to spend time with each other. They are willing to forego some things that they might otherwise have in order to maximize the time they can be together. One of the spouses, for instance, might refuse a promotion that would mean a greatly increased amount of time away from home. Their preference for being together is not based upon a loss of individuality, or upon a conflict-free relationship. They have many of the same problems that people in other marriages have. But they do not fight over trivial issues. They handle conflict in a constructive fashion (see chapter 7). They work through difficulties and problems and their relationship is strengthened by the effort.

THE TOTAL MARRIAGE

This union is similar to the vital marriage, except that it is even more encompassing of each spouse's life. The sharing is nearly complete in the total marriage. The relationship is quite open; the spouses do not "play games" with each other. There is little conflict. The differences that arise are handled quickly through compromise or through one of the spouses giving in. It doesn't matter to them that one or the other sometimes gives in on an issue because the most important thing in their lives is their relationship itself.

The total marriage, according to Cuber and Harroff, is very uncommon. But there are some, and they can endure. The spouses in such a marriage seem to have no private aspect at all to their lives. Everything is shared, everything is done as a pair, and each spouse prefers such an arrangement.

Most of the happy couples in our sample have a vital marriage. Very few, if any, have a total marriage. We would agree that this kind of marriage is rare. In fact, a total marriage raises the question of the true well-being of the individuals involved. As we shall discuss in chapter 6, one of the tasks of a meaningful relationship is how to maintain both individuality and union. Roughly, then, our typology relates to that of Cuber and Harroff as follows:

Both spouses unhappy   Conflict-habituated or Devitalized
One spouse unhappy   Passive-Congenial
Both spouses happy   Vital or Total

Since the remainder of this book deals with aspects of the lives of those in vital marriages, we shall not discuss them further here. Let us, instead, turn to the interesting question of why people remain in a less-than-satisfying relationship over an extended period of time.

THE ENDURANCE OF UNHAPPINESS

Since Americans tend to view happiness as one of their rightful expectations of the marital state, why do some people remain in a union that is unsatisfying to them for decades? One of the questions we asked of all of our couples, including those who said they were unhappy, was to identify, from a list of thirty-nine factors, those that were most important in explaining why their marriage had endured. Among our mixed couples (one happy and one unhappy spouse), all of the factors named by at least 10% of the respondents are shown in Table 3.1 (most respondents gave more than one answer).

The most frequent reason given, by both happy and unhappy spouses, for staying together was a belief that marriage involves a long-term commitment. For the unhappy spouses, the second most common reason was the classic "for the sake of the children," followed by liking the mate as a person and then by viewing marriage as a sacred institution. For the happy spouses, viewing the mate as a best friend was the second most frequent choice, followed by the children, liking the mate as a person, and agreement on aims and goals in life.

There is a difference, then, in the perceptions of those who are happy versus those who are unhappy in the mixed marriages. While both see commitment as very important, happy spouses tend to identify their positive feelings about their mates as important, while unhappy spouses tend to focus on their concerns about the children.

There were a scattering of other reasons given by those in mixed marriages. A few happy and unhappy spouses said that one reason was their desire to make the marriage succeed. Some of the factors named by one or two happy spouses that were not identified by any of the unhappy spouses included engaging in shared activities,

Table 3.1

Reasons for Staying Together in Mixed Marriages

Reason	% of Respondents	
	happy	unhappy
marriage involves a long-term commitment	34.4	31.2
my mate is my best friend	25.0	
the children	18.8	25.0
I like my mate as a person	15.6	15.6
marriage is a sacred institution		12.5
agreement on aims and goals in life	12.5	

viewing the mate as more interesting than when first married, and agreeing on major decisions.

Some respondents indicated that none of the thirty-nine factors we offered them best explained the stability of their marriages. A physician who is unhappy in his marriage of 32 years said that a divorce would simply cost him too much. An engineer said that a divorce would hinder him in his profession and, moreover, "I'm comfortable with her; she's predictable" (this is the classic passive-congenial match). A couple of respondents admitted that they stayed in their marriages because of the financial security they had. Jeff, a counselor married for 22 years, said that his parents and church were both strong influences in his decision to stay with his wife. He feared disapproval and rejection by his intimates if he broke up with his wife. He was also afraid of being alone. And a housewife with five children pointed out that the social stigma of being divorced in her family would be worse than staying in her unhappy marriage.

Clearly, an important factor in the stability of the mixed marriage is an acceptance of social values and norms, which are reinforced by pressures from family members and religious ideologies. The commitment to marriage in such a case does not stem from any gratification the unhappy individual is receiving, but from a determined acceptance of the notion that marriage is sacred and that those who enter that holy state do so for better or worse even if the great bulk of times are the worst of times.

Parental concerns also enter in to reinforce the need to maintain the marriage. Geraldine was married for more than 30 years before she finally divorced her husband. Those 30 years were a long story of verbal abuse and frustration over her husband's erratic behavior. Finally, her commitment to the match was irreparably broken when she was assaulted one night and her husband refused to take her to the hospital for medical attention. She left and never returned. We asked her why she had stayed with him for so long. She replied:

> What other choice did I have? We were married during the Great Depression. When the children started coming I needed him for financial support. He drove me crazy with his financial schemes that never left us with much money, but at least we did have enough for the necessities. I was ready to leave him when I discovered that I was pregnant with my last child. I didn't think that it was right to raise a child without a father even if I could have supported us. So I stayed on. But when I was assaulted, I didn't have to worry about a small child having a father anymore. That was the end.

Staying together for the sake of the children is viewed by many Americans as more of a foolish decision than a noble gesture. Yet there is a parental wisdom to the decision, as long as the marital relationship is not a destructive one. Children raised in stepfamilies can do as well as those who grow up with their natural mothers and fathers. But children reared in a single-parent home are more likely to get involved in a variety of problems. One study of more than 1,300 young people in Minnesota, aged 19 to 34, reported that those who had been reared in one-parent families were more likely to have lower incomes, more likely to be on welfare, and more likely to be divorced than those raised by two parents.[4] A study that involved a representative sample of adolescents in the nation reported that youth raised by mothers alone, as compared to those reared by both natural parents, are more likely to get involved in various kinds of deviant behavior.[5] In particular, the youth from the mother-only homes were more likely to: have contact with the law, be arrested, be disciplined at school, be truant, smoke regularly, and run away. Finally, a survey of over 800 adults found that abusive punishment is twice as likely in a single-parent as a two-parent household.[6] Those parents who endure some unhappiness with their marriage in order to maintain a stable home for the children may indeed be sacrificing some personal gratification for the well-being of the children.

We should note that the future of a marriage which is held

together for the sake of the children is precarious. As in the case of Geraldine, the marriage may finally dissolve when the children are grown. One housewife in our sample who has been married for 26 years made this interesting observation:

> The coming of children made us both happier. There was a low point when I lost 34 pounds and felt desirable, but found myself ignored more. The weight loss gave me enough self-esteem to get help as to why we were still having problems . . . I have three years of weekly visits with a psychiatrist. If I had visited the psychiatrist before we had our children, it's likely we would have been divorced. After our children leave home, I wonder what will happen. I'll cross that bridge when I get to it.

Finally, we should keep in mind that only one member of the mixed marriage is unhappy. Are both spouses aware of how each other feels? Some of the unhappy spouses indicated that they knew their unhappiness was not shared by their spouse. Some of the happy spouses were clearly unaware, or at least refused to admit that they were aware, of living with an unhappy mate. But at times there are intimations that the happy spouse knows how the other feels. One husband noted that the children had changed his and his wife's lives dramatically.

> Our schedules have become very much a dictator of our actions. We rarely have time to ourselves. Others have parents or relatives nearby to babysit. We don't have that luxury. While this has possibly hurt our relationship as man and wife, it has allowed us to be a strong, closely-knit family. This is what holds our marriage together.

One hears in the above account a sense of concern about the marital relationship and, at the same time, a quick denial that that relationship is really threatened. A good many of the happy people in mixed marriages undoubtedly protect themselves by denial of the problem.

At any rate, the fact that only one spouse is somewhat unhappy can make the home a more tolerable situation for the children, who are less likely to be aware of the unhappiness, and can also intensify the pressures to keep the marriage intact. The unhappy spouse faces a disturbing question: is it easier to bear my own unhappiness or to bear the trauma that I will create in my spouse, my children, and our friends and family by breaking up the marriage? The unhappy spouse is likely to choose the former, and to seek alternative gratifications in a career or activities away from home. An illustration of this is a wife of 26 years who is "a little unhappy" in her marriage:

Our problem has been sexual and yet we are still married because something in our background has contributed to our staying together. I have been so sexually frustrated that I wanted to do something to help others. I became a volunteer sex educator for Planned Parenthood. It's interesting to look back 26 years ago and realize there was no one I could have talked to, to help me at that time. Now we have sex therapists in most large cities. I was born too soon, or should I say my husband was. His strong religious background—his father and both grandfathers were ministers—was to his disadvantage sexually.

The situation is somewhat different where both spouses are unhappy, as shown by the reasons they give for staying together (Table 3.2). Again, the emphasis is on commitment to marriage, which is frequently viewed as a sacred institution. Unhappy couples also pointed to their belief that enduring marriages are important to society as a factor in their mutual stability. Their responses begin to sound as if they are desperately seeking justifications for their

Table 3.2

Reasons for Staying Together in Unhappy Marriages

Reason	% of Respondents
marriage involves a long-term commitment	52.6
children	47.4
marriage is a sacred institution	21.1
enduring marriages are important to society	15.8
my mate is my best friend	10.5

unhappiness by stressing the importance of stability in marriage. It is interesting that a few of them still said that their mates were their best friends. This may sound strange if they are unhappy. However, recall the story of Edna and Sam from chapter 1. Once when talking with Edna we asked her why she stayed with Sam. She thought about the question a moment, began to weep softly, and said: "He's all I've got." In spite of her unhappiness with him, he was the only "friend" that she had at the time. But while a marriage is more likely to be happy when the spouses view each other as best friends, a happy marriage requires more than friendship.

As in the mixed marriages, our unhappy couples gave various other reasons for staying together. In two instances, the bond was one of health—the couple stayed together because one was quite ill and needed care from the other. For example, a husband told us that he had to care for almost all of his wife's needs. He was unhappy, but would not leave her because it would make him feel guilty. "What would become of her?" he asked. "What would she do for money? What would happen to her emotionally?"

In some cases, people settle into the rut of unhappiness with their marriage and find it easier to slide along in the rut than to go through the trauma of change. "We've been together too long to get divorced now," said a retired blue-collar worker who has been married for 37 years. "Why bother?" In some cases, the marriage is a devitalized one—the slipping into a rut after an initial period of happiness. A wife who said she was "fairly unhappy" in her 17-year marriage said: "We were happiest in the first few years. Then things went downhill somewhat and have stayed the same ever since."

Finally, family and religious pressures come to bear upon the unhappy couples. A housewife of 18 years said: "We are Catholic and do not believe in divorce. If all people remained married and raised their children properly there would be less crime in the world."

There is a note of pathos in many of the comments. The unhappy couples frequently present themselves as those who are caught up in a web of sadness from which they cannot possibly extricate themselves. A few droplets of hope may fall into the arid words that describe their marriage. But the dominant sense that one gets from them is resignation:

> People today divorce when things go wrong that is part of life. Marriage is a duty. It's not necessarily supposed to be happy all the time. (married 15 years)

My marriage is stable because of family, society, religion, kids, and money. We have a large family now, and my wife wants still more children. Because of that, I had to give up the career I really wanted. I went into a business that gives me a lot of money, more than I could have earned otherwise. But the job is boring and not challenging and not the career I wanted or was trained for. But by the time my children are raised it will be too late to change. (married 19 years)

We've stayed together because of tradition. That's what I think marriage is about. I believe in keeping the marriage intact. Through thick and thin and ups and downs. And hope that it will always get better. (married 30 years)

Children make obligations that you wouldn't have if you were single. I was married once before for a couple of years. That made me try harder in my second marriage. I couldn't tolerate the idea of a second failure. At my age, I would hesitate to make a change even if I am unhappy. (married 38 years)

HOW MANY CHANCES?

What are the possibilities for those in less-than-satisfying marriages? How many chances does one have to reach the ideal of a stable and happy marriage? The high divorce rates suggest that Americans do maintain high expectations for their marriages and that these expectations are not being fulfilled.[7] They are free to divorce without stigma, and they do so in considerable number. But is there any likelihood that the second or third marriage will prove any more successful than the first?

Most Americans are willing to gamble that they can eventually achieve the ideal. Over 85% of all those who get divorced eventually remarry.[8] About one out of every four people who divorce will remarry within a year. Whether those who remarry have any greater chance of a stable, happy union is a matter of some debate among the experts. Some claim that there is no greater chance of breakup, while others argue that the divorce rate among second marriages is higher than that of first marriages.[9]

We cannot resolve that issue, but our data do indicate one interesting fact—second marriages can last and can be either satisfying or unhappy. Among our respondents, about 11% of those in happy marriages, 7% of those in mixed marriages, and 31% of those in unhappy matches indicated that they had been previously married. Our sample of unhappy marriages is too small to make any firm conclusions, but if our respondents reflect a general pattern, a second marriage that lasts is more likely than a lasting first marriage to be unsatisfactory.

We asked those who had been married before to indicate what, if anything, they had learned from their first marriage. The majority gave a simple answer—nothing. Or as one man put it more forcefully, "Not a damned thing." The answer undoubtedly reflected a certain amount of bitterness with the first marriage and a certain unwillingness to discuss or think about it. A few people suggested that the first, unsuccessful match had at least taught them what to value in a mate and a relationship.

A remarriage, of course, involves certain challenges and difficulties which are not present in a first marriage. Cox has noted five pitfalls that confront a marriage between two people who are divorced.[10] First, the spouses may have a problem of self-esteem stemming from their failure to make a success of their first marriages. Second, people who are divorced are less likely to be willing to tolerate a second, unsatisfying marriage. They probably would not be willing, like the respondents discussed above, to grimly accept an unhappy relationship. They, after all, have been through the process of divorce once and know that they can survive the breakup.

Third, the relationship with the divorced spouses will not be completely over. If children are involved, this will be particularly acute, as we shall discuss below. But even apart from children, and even if there is no financial support involved, two people who live together for a period of time leave their marks on each other in numerous ways. An invidious comparison between the present and past spouse, a thoughtful word or act for a former spouse, behavior that a former spouse appreciated—these are but a few of the many things that can lead to jealousy or conflict.

Fourth, people may expect the marriage to fail. After all, the first marriage failed. Is there any reason to expect that the person can do better this time? There is a certain amount of "folk wisdom" that leads people to expect a divorced person to continue in the same, inept paths of behavior that led to the failure of the first marriage. And if people around you expect you to fail, it is easier to give up the struggle that inevitably marks the building of a successful relationship.

Finally, children pose special problems for the remarriage.[11] Each of the children probably lost an important primary relationship. A child may be angry about the loss, and his or her anger can be directed against the stepparent. Furthermore, the lost parent may maintain contact with the child, which can help or can intensify the problems of adjustment with the reconstituted family. A child may compete with a stepparent for the attention and affection of the natural parent. The stepparent role itself is ambiguous, which can lead to various problems as the adult and the child attempt to adjust to the situation. Is the stepparent to be like a natural parent, or like a friend, or like a teacher? All of these problems are only intensified when there are children in the home for both of the spouses.

In spite of the potential problems, many people in second marriages report a high degree of satisfaction. The 31% of the unhappy respondents in our sample who indicated a previous marriage underscore the fact that it may be no better the second time around. But the 11% of our happy respondents who were previously married demonstrate that a second match can be both stable and rewarding. The question is, how does a couple go about building a long-term, satisfying marriage? The answer will require the remainder of the book.

FOOTNOTES

1. John F. Cuber, with Peggy B. Harroff, *The Significant Americans: A Study of Sexual Behavior Among the Affluent* (New York: Appleton-Century, 1965).
2. *Ibid.*, p. 44.
3. *Ibid.*, p. 50.
4. Reported in *Psychology Today*, February, 1985, p. 16.
5. Sanford M. Dornbusch *et al*, "Single Parents, Extended Households, and the Control of Adolescents," *Child Development* 56 (April, 1985):326–41.
6. William H. Sack, Robert Mason, and James E. Higgins, "The Single-Parent Family and Abusive Child Punishment," *American Journal of Orthopsychiatry* 55 (April, 1985): 252–59.
7. Frank D. Cox, *Human Intimacy: Marriage, the Family and Its Meaning*, 3rd ed. (St. Paul, Minn.: West Publishing Co., 1984), p. 522.
8. F. Philip Rice, *Contemporary Marriage* (Boston: Allyn & Bacon, 1983), p. 297.
9. Rice, *op. cit.*, p. 297; Paul C. Glick, "Marriage, Divorce, and Living Arrangements," *Journal of Family Issues* 5 (March, 1984):7–26.
10. Cox, *op. cit.*, p. 515.
11. E. B. Visher and J. Visher, *Stepfamilies: A Guide to Working with Stepparents and Stepchildren* (New York: Brunner/Mazel, 1979).

Chapter 4
'Til Death Do Us Part:
The Role of Commitment

"I'll tell you why we've stayed together," said a Texas woman who has been married for 18 years. "I'm just too damned stubborn to give up." It was her way of saying that she was committed to her marriage. And she, like many of our long-term, happily-married couples, believed that too many young Americans take the notion of commitment too lightly.

Do Americans have a commitment problem? Are they unwilling to link themselves faithfully to another individual until death do them part? Some experts think so. As William Kilpatrick argued, the breakdown of marriages and friendships is not due to a "lack of human relationship expertise. There is plenty of that around. Unfortunately, in all their concern with sensitivity and expressiveness, the experts fail to talk about the one thing that does make a relationship last: commitment."[1] Moreover, Kilpatrick says, commitment is something that people today shy away from. People do not want to choose. They do not want to choose because that means that they will have to forego those things not chosen. People prefer to "taste all possibilities without ever having to choose among them."[2]

On the other side of the argument, Daniel Yankelovich claims that Americans are developing a new "ethic of commitment."[3] That means that they are turning away from a preoccupation with self and exploring a "connectedness" with their world. The turning towards commitment may involve a connectedness with people, objects, beliefs, or any number of things. One of the more important manifestations of the ethic of commitment is a hunger for more meaningful personal relationships. Yankelovich noted that his surveys show an increasing proportion of Americans who indicate that they feel a need for being an integral part of some group. They are, in increasing numbers, committing themselves in an effort to satisfy their felt need for community.

If Kilpatrick is correct, Americans face troubled years in their marriages. If Yankelovich is correct, and if the trend continues, it bodes well for the future of marriage. For, as Kilpatrick insisted, commitment is one of the foremost requirements of an enduring marriage. As we have seen, commitment by two people can maintain a union for decades even when the spouses are unhappy with each other and dissatisfied with their relationship. Both happy and unhappy spouses in our sample agreed overwhelmingly that marriage involves a long-term commitment (Table 4.1). While, therefore, we cannot answer the question of the extent of Americans' willingness to commit themselves, we can underscore the importance of that commitment to an enduring union. Furthermore, our couples gave us important insights into such matters as the meaning and consequences of being committed in marriage.

THE MEANING OF COMMITMENT

Naomi Quinn interviewed a number of people about their marriages, then analyzed the transcripts to try to get at the meaning of such abstracct terms as commitment.[4] She found that commitment can have somewhat different meanings to different people. In the context of marriage, the term seems to have three distinct meanings to Americans: promise, dedication, and attachment. The meanings are related. Commitment means a promise or pledge to engage in something that will be difficult over the long run. It is, after all, for better or for worse. To commit means to promise to be dedicated or devoted to a joint goal of staying together and forming a meaningful family unit. To have a joint goal is to say that the two people must each make the promise and devote themselves to pursuing the goal. And that means attachment to each other. "The attachment is not intellectual, as commitment to an idea can be, or contractual, as commitment to an obligation; its overriding sense is rather that of emotional attachment."[5]

The findings of Quinn are consistent with the statements that our happily-married respondents made about their commitment. People do not necessarily use the terms promise, dedication, and attachment, but the meanings are there. A wife of 26 years said: "I believe when you enter into marriage, it is a lifetime commitment, not something you change at every whim." Another said that commitment "is a promise that you'll always be there." A husband expressed his commitment in terms of "strong feelings about

Table 4.1

Percent of Responses to: "Marriage Is a Long-Term Commitment"

	Happy	Mixed	Unhappy
Strongly Agree	79.6	56.2	44.7
Agree	18.6	37.5	47.4
Neutral	1.2	6.2	5.3
Disagree	0.6	0	2.6
Strongly Disagree	0	0	0
	100.0%	99.9%	100.0%

keeping the marriage vows." Mona, a computer programmer who has been married for 30 years, observed:

> I think we always felt our relationship with each other came first. Parenting was important. And sometimes physically came first. But our primary emotional commitment was to each other.

And David, happily married for 31 years, expressed his views of commitment in terms of feelings and attachment:

> Originally it was "chemistry" that brought us together. Then it was a sense of duty and obligation. And finally it is friendship and a lot of memories and other ties holding us together. I have a very strong sense of commitment.

Commitment involves a promise of dedication to a relationship in which there is an emotional attachment to another person who has made the same promise.

COMMITTED TO WHAT?

Quinn found that commitment in marriage is primarily an emotional attachment to a person rather than a contractual obligation. But we found that the sense of contractual obligation also exists. Among our long-term couples, whether happy or not, commitment includes a dedication to the spouse, but it also includes a dedication to the institution of marriage. That is, our couples take seriously the notion that marriage is not to be entered into lightly, that one has a kind of social obligation to the institution itself as well as a personal obligation to the spouse. Both kinds of commitment are important.

Clearly, they are committed to their spouses. Like David, when they talk about commitment they do so in the context of their relationship. And for the happy couples, the emotional attachment to another person is the dominant meaning of commitment. For example, a husband pointed out that to him commitment means that "the door is open and you choose to stay." And a wife said that she didn't even like the word "commitment." For her, it has a negative connotation. "It seems to mean that you *must* stay together. I stay with my husband because I want to, not because I have to."

However, when asked why her marriage had endured, the same woman said: "People our age don't just walk out on a marriage. We were taught that you just don't do that." In other words, she was committed to the institution of marriage as well as to her husband. Such commitment is reflected in the responses to the questions of how important enduring marriages are to a stable society and whether marriage is a sacred institution. The majority of all respondents, including 80% of those happily married, agreed that marriage is a sacred institution. And 92% of the happily married, and over three-fourths of those in mixed and unhappy marriages agreed with the statement that enduring marriages are important to a stable society.

Other researchers have reported similar results. Roberts noted, in his study of 50 couples married an average of 55.5 years, that most of his respondents did not even consider divorce as an option.[6] A few smilingly remarked that they might consider murder but not divorce. Similarly, Sporakowski and Hughston studied couples married at least 50 years.[7] Among other things, they asked their respondents to define marriage, and found that both husbands and wives gave "forever" as an important part of the meaning of marriage. For them, "marriage" was virtually equivalent to "commitment."

There are, then, at least three kinds of commitment that we have discovered. First, there is the commitment to a happy marriage. Sandra, the young wife we discussed in chapter 1, represents this kind of commitment. Sandra believed that marriages should last a lifetime, but only if both people are happy in the marriage. When she was no longer happy with her husband, she felt no more commitment.

Second, there is a commitment to marriage itself. The unhappy spouses we discussed in the last chapter had this kind of commitment. They were determined to last it out regardless of their personal feelings. Because of such things as their belief in the obligatory nature of the wedding vows, their sense of the importance of a stable family to the children, and their unwillingness to offend members of the family, they endured an unhappy union. Their commitment was not really to the spouse but to the institution of marriage. As we shall discuss below, had they been truly committed to their spouses, they would not have allowed the marriage to continue on in the mire of unhappiness.

Third, there is a commitment to both marriage and the spouse. The happily-married couples represent this kind of commitment. We will explore the meaning and implications of that twofold commitment in the following sections.

In an enduring and happy marriage, there is a commitment both to the spouse and to the institution of marriage.

THE SOURCES OF COMMITMENT

Why do people commit themselves in marriage? Those in happy marriages, of course, do not have much of a problem in committing themselves, or in perceiving themselves as committed. They are committed to that which is meaningful and gratifying to them. As we shall see in the next chapter, they like their spouses and would want to know them and be friends with them even if they were not married to them. There is an interaction between their feelings and their commitment: the feelings reinforce the commitment and the commitment, in turn, helps maintain the feelings.

In addition, however, the happy couples indicated that they believed in the importance of a stable family life. That belief comes in part from an acceptance of family values, which, in turn, tend to reflect social norms. Historically, Americans have viewed marriage as a lifetime commitment. The traditional marriage vows themselves underscore this in the phrase " 'til death do us part." Some of our respondents pointed out that they had learned and accepted the notion of lifetime commitment from their families. A midwestern wife of 37 years said: "We went into marriage without considering that there might be a possibility of divorce. We both came from very conservative, stable families and considered that the way to be." And a California woman who had a happy, 41-year marriage noted: "We were brought up that you had to stay married no matter what. We never really considered that there might be another option."

Religious beliefs and involvement may reinforce the belief in marital commitment. As noted above, the great majority of our respondents agreed that marriage is a sacred institution. Some specifically linked the sacredness of marriage with their own responsibility to be faithful to death. Bill is a salesman who has been married for 15 years. He sees his relationship with his wife as a spiritual matter:

> From the beginning of our relationship, my wife and I felt as if God brought us together at the right time to be together. We took our commitment seriously, not just to each other but the commitment that God expected from us to work together and make it work.

Similarly, a husband of 41 years said: "I've always lived according to God and the church, and believe that it is God's will to obey the marriage vows until death."

Both family values and religious beliefs are supported by observing the consequences of divorce. "I think that seeing the effect that divorce," observed one wife, "even friendly divorce, has on young children has made me see the need to make sure that children are given a stable home life." Those who know the trauma experienced by adults and children when divorce occurs (and few Americans are untouchd by divorce among family or friends), have a living illustration of the value of the norms and beliefs that stress family stability.

Another reason for commitment given by our respondents is a belief that strong families are necessary for a stable society. As a husband put it:

> The family is the most important institution in a stable and healthy and happy society. The family and all of its members make it possible for a society, a civilization, to grow and to develop into something wholesome and productive. Destroy the family and you destroy civilization and progress.

While not all of them phrased it in such terms, the great bulk of our respondents agreed that stable families are necessary for a stable society.

Commitment to marriage on the basis of its value to society should not be taken as an expression of pure altruism. It is not that people are sacrificing themselves on the altar of societal survival. Rather, they believe that the individual will maximize his or her well-being when there is social well-being. Americans sense a need for a stable social order if they as individuals are to have happy and secure lives, and they see family stability as one of the more important contributors to social stability.

Marital commitment is strengthened by a belief in the importance of a stable family life.

IMPLICATIONS OF COMMITMENT

Exactly what does it mean to say that someone is committed to another person and to marriage? Commitment, like marriage itself, is not merely a solution but a task. As one of our wives succinctly put it, "Marriage is work." And a husband noted that marriage "requires a lot of work from both partners. It is *not* something that just happens." That is, it is not the commitment that resolves marital problems. Rather, commitment provides the necessary context for the resolution of problems. For that commitment implies that the individual is willing to set out on a particular course and resolutely stay with that course by confronting and dealing with all obstacles and deterrents. A marriage and family therapist, James L. Framo, has written: "Everyone knows that marriage is an impossible state."[8] He goes on to ask how two people can possibly relate to each other with compatibility when they come from different backgrounds in which they have learned differing notions of proper thinking and behavior. A significant part of the answer begins with commitment, which means a willingness to endure troubled times and to work through the plexus of difficulties that inevitably assault every married couple.

In talking about their commitment, our respondents emphasized time and again the importance of working through troubled days and problematic situations, and the fact that commitment to them meant a willingness to do that work. It is at this point that their commitment differs from that of the unhappy spouses. The latter were willing to endure the problems. But those who are committed to another person as well as to a marriage are unwilling to allow that other person, much less themselves, to continue in an unsatisfying relationship. To the happily-married, commitment is to the well-being of the other, not to an endurance contest. Unhappy spouses may hope that it is true that time heals all wounds, and that ultimately the relationship will get better or at least more tolerable. But happy couples try to resolve problems rather than outlast them.

One wife told us that she and her husband reached a point in their marriage where they began drifting apart. They both were involved in their work, and eventually both became involved with someone else. The day that each discovered the infidelity of the other was a day of mutual shock. Each felt betrayed, even though each had been a betrayer. Their initial reaction was to agree to seek a divorce. Then they reflected on their situation, their feelings about each other, and their commitments. They decided to attack the problems in their relationship. Eventually, they worked through the problems, forgave each other, and are again experiencing the deep love that bound them together in an earlier part of their marriage.

Some of our respondents feel that young people are unwilling to be committed to that extent today, that spouses now are too willing, like Sandra, to leave each other rather than face up to the inevitable rough times of marriage:

> We've remained married because forty years ago our peer group just did. We worked our way through problems that today we might walk away from. Our marriage is firm and filled with respect and love, but it took time and work. In a marriage today, we might have separated. I'm glad we didn't. I can't emphasize this too strongly. I have two children who divorced. They are still searching for a magical something that isn't obtainable in the real world. Marriage grows through working out problems and going on. Our marriage took forty years and we are still learning.

Similarly, another wife talked about five years of serious problems in her marriage. But: "Because I believe marriage is a long-term commitment, there would be few things a couple couldn't work out if given time and not too much interference from friends and relatives."

The perception of younger couples as being less willing to confront and work through difficulties may be accurate. Our own discussions with younger couples indicate that the thought of their own divorce is less disquieting to them than it would be to the long-term couples in our sample. For example, when we asked a young woman who had been married four years how she felt about divorce if she and her husband had serious problems (they did not have any at the time), she reflected for a few moments, then said:

> Yes, I would consider divorce. I never thought about it before, but I realize that I have a much different attitude than my parents have. I think that they believe that they're married for life whatever happens. But I don't think that I would stay with my husband if things really got bad. I know that divorce is always an option.

The point is, according to our couples, that things *will* get bad. How long would that young woman endure the bad times before she opted for divorce? How strenuously would she be willing to work at resolving the problems before she sought release from the marriage? Commitment means a willingness, indeed a determination, to overcome problems rather than to be overcome by them.

"Determination" is a part of commitment because the individuals will not always feel like engaging in the task of problem solving. In other words, commitment means behaving at times in a way that is contrary to the individual's feelings and preferences. One husband said that he would go to almost any lengths to make his relationship with his wife succeed. But, he noted, he hadn't always felt that way. It was his commitment that led him to continue to struggle with the problems even when his feelings kept enticing him away from the battle. Thus, there is a rational element in commitment that may have to deal with emotions that contradict the course of behavior dictated by the reason. As Bill, a manager, said of his more than 25-year marriage:

> I feel myself extremely fortunate. If ever a marriage was made in heaven, it's mine. But it isn't always sweetness and light. We've had our rough times. When those times come, I have a dialogue with myself. I have to keep talking with myself so that my feelings don't push me into doing or saying something stupid. There have been time when I felt like giving up and walking out. But then I remind myself that I'm committed to this marriage.

Of course, it requires more than willingness or determination to work through problems. For commitment to be effective (that is, to lead to a long-term, gratifying union), there must be certain other skills and qualities in the relationship. We will explore these in subsequent chapters. Here, we might mention two that were pointed out by our respondents when talking about their own commitment. One is patience. We raised the question above of how long one should endure troubled times, how strenuously one should work at resolving problems. Will those in our sample who have been unhappily married for 15 years or more ever get out of the morass of misery? How does one know when one is merely going through a troubled time in an otherwise gratifying marriage versus when one is caught up in a tangled web of a joyless relationship that will never change?

There is no simple answer to the questions. Those who struggle with them should work them out with a counselor or therapist. It is clear from our respondents, however, that some relationships can be less than satisfactory for quite a few years, and finally blossom into a happy union. Winnie is "extremely happy" now in her 26-year marriage, but that happiness came very slowly:

As I recall the first ten years of our marriage, I think of myself as somebody else's. I was somebody's wife, somebody's mother, and so on. After 10 years, I began to be emotionally depressed, and this worsened with passing time. I can remember desperately wanting to commit suicide, but couldn't because there would be no one to care for the children. My husband never ceased to love me, even though I was a very unlovable person.

After about 15 years of marriage, Winnie had a religious experience that brought her out of her depression. Finally, she says, "I was able to return the love that my family had so faithfully given me." Both Winnie and her husband indicated that they were unhappy in their marriage during the years of her depression. But even in his unhappiness, he was obviously able to convey to her a sense of his love and patient support. For some of our couples, the willingness and determination to work through problems did not mean a few hours or days or weeks, but a number of years.

Another implication of commitment is the acceptance of the other. "We both had a life-time commitment," said a wife of 35 years. "So in the first ten years we both did a lot of adjusting and compromising, and learned to accept each other's differences." Our couples indicated that they lived by the principles expressed in the prayer advocated by Alcoholics Anonymous; they changed what they could, accepted what they could not change, and tried to have the wisdom to know the difference between the two. They accepted their spouses as they were. They said in effect: I am committed to you as you are now; my commitment is not to the person you will become or to the person that I hope you become, but to you as you are. Such commitment must be a reciprocal affair, of course. Each spouse accepts the other. Each will, as we shall see in chapter 8, work to change the other, but will also accept that which cannot be changed. The commitment is to the actual person as he or she is, not to an ideal mate that exists only in fantasy.

Commitment means the willingness and determination to work through troubled times.

Commitment implies patience and acceptance, qualities which are necessary for commitment to be effective.

CONSEQUENCES OF COMMITMENT

If we appear to have drawn a somewhat somber portrait of commitment thus far, we should note that, according to our couples, commitment has a number of consequences which are very positive and desirable.

An Enhanced Quality in the Relationship

The business of working through difficulties is not merely a grim task to be endured. Rather, difficult times have their own value for the couple. It isn't that they enjoy the difficulties, but that they can look back on them and see the ways in which their relationship was enriched and strengthened as a result of working together through the problems. June, a midwestern mother of two grown children, is "extremely happy" in her marriage of 35 years, and can see now how she and her husband benefited from their commitment to work through difficulties:

> For the first five years we were making adjustments and learning to cooperate on problems. Over the years, our relationship has gradually improved and our understanding of each other has deepened as we weathered the problems of raising a family together. During stressful times my spouse and I have supported each other, so that even having problems has strengthened our relationship.

Another wife, married 15 years, talked about problems with children and money, and the value of confronting and dealing jointly with those problems:

> Our biggest challenge over the years is raising three children comfortably and keeping our sanity. We began to see us disagreeing about the children. We discussed our feelings about how the children should be disciplined and came up with a mutual set of rules. Another problem was money. My husband is a school teacher and doesn't make enough money to keep the children fed and clothed. So I stepped in and went back to work part-time. We complement each other by helping each other get through troubled times without letting either of us tackle all the burdens. I think these problems have increased

our relationship by making us work together with no one taking the blame.

Working through difficult times can lead to a stronger and more meaningful relationship.

Security

To know that your mate is committed to you is to have a sense of security in a turbulent world. There are various kinds of security, all of which are important. But our respondents stressed the emotional security which they have because they know that their spouses are committed to their marriages. "I always feel that he's there if I need him," said one wife. "Security is important. He's dependable. I can count on him more than anybody else I know." Another wife, when asked if there was anything that had not been discussed that she felt was important in her marriage, responded: "Just that I know I can depend on my husband, know that he sincerely cares for me in spite of my faults and shortcomings."

Such security is liberating. An individual who always lives at the edge of financial problems may get fixated on money and find his or her life consumed by an effort to gain some measure of security. Similarly, an individual who feels that his or her relationships are held together by fragile bonds may get fixated on continually seeking reassurance. Security, on the other hand, liberates the individual to not only enjoy the relationship at a level otherwise impossible, but also to pursue other, meaningful activities. This point was stressed by Kathy, a Georgia wife who has been married for 29 years:

> We take our marriage for granted now. We never talk about it. I am secure there. My husband is not going to abandon me, nor I him. Continually examining the marriage as magazines and questionnaires suggest seems to me to show that you are looking for some fault. When the marriage is secure, the couple can think of other people and other activities. This is what I do now. My marriage gives me a companion. I am free in its security and can grow in any other direction I want.

A number of our respondents expressed this security in terms of trust. Commitment appears to generate trust.[11] The deeper the commitment each spouse perceives in the other, the greater the trust. Mutual trust means that each spouse is secure in the relationship so that little energy is wasted on jealousy, suspicion, and behavior aimed at eliciting reassurance. It isn't that the couple is totally free of these problems, but that they are of minimal importance. "We are not jealous of each other," said one wife:

> That doesn't mean that there is never a flash of emotion that could turn into jealousy. But we also know that that flash of emotion is our own problem to deal with and is not our mate's fault. My husband is true to me as I am to him. We have such a wonderful marriage that neither one would put it in jeopardy. We make ourselves vulnerable to each other, and have the trust that the other will cherish that vulnerability.

Commitment allows each spouse to have the security necessary to develop a more meaningful union and to grow as an individual.

Support

One of the consistent findings of research is that supportive interpersonal relationships can minimize the deleterious effects of stress. The other side of the coin is that the lack of such relationships means vulnerability to the consequences of stress. The stress can be of diverse kinds from varied sources. For example, people who lived near the Three Mile Island nuclear power plant in Pennsylvania were evacuated when the plant suffered a near meltdown. The experience was highly stressful, even a year after the disaster. But those residents who had a social support network had fewer psychological and behavioral symptoms of stress than the others.[9] Similarly, two researchers studied thousands of Israeli men over a five-year period to try and determine how angina pectoris develops. They found that one of the better predictors of those men who were high risks was the answer to a question: "Does your wife show you her love?" Those who answered "no" were more likely to develop the heart disorder.[10]

A happy marriage, then, in which both partners are committed, provides a known source of support in the face of various problems. "To know that you have someone to love you," said a man happily married for 33 years, "and can depend on no matter what problems may arise is really important. It's like having a crutch under a broken leg that you rely on to support you." Another husband put it this way: "I think that we feel that we are more or less in this together and we are the only support we have and can depend on. All in all, we are one." And still another husband testified:

I know that whatever I do, whatever happens to me, she will continue to love me. Once I came home to find a letter that was a harsh setback to my career aspirations. I was deeply disappointed by it. She couldn't be there when I got home. But there was the letter with a note from her that said, "Just remember. I love you." I've never forgotten that. No matter how frustrating things get with my work, I know that I have the support of her love. And that's what really matters.

Commitment means that each spouse has the interpersonal support necessary to deal with the stresses of life.

Survival

Because of their security, because of the known support that they have, our respondents feel that they can survive any kind of problem. They indicated that their relationships enabled them to effectively deal with all sorts of adversity without being financially, physically, interpersonally, or emotionally crippled. In some cases, the survival was the result of simple support. A husband who has been married 27 years said that a low point occurred in the marriage around the second year. He had just been discharged from the military and their first child was born. "Things were a bit difficult. She helped me through this period with her understanding."

In some cases, the survival is financial, and it demands a certain amount of sacrifice. Hank, very happy with his 20-year marriage, told how his wife worked with him to make a career change possible:

My wife was extremely supportive when I gave up a good paying job in printing to move to the West Coast and start over with my brother in computers. The children were young and we had terrible financial problems. She would babysit six or seven other kids besides our four in order to help make ends meet. She never made me feel bad for earning less and she has always encouraged me and believed in me more than I did myself. Now I am in management and have a good paying job due to her many sacrifices.

Sometimes the adversity involves physical as well as other problems. Philip, married for 46 years, said that his wife had to nurse him through complete paralysis shortly after they were married. She then supported him for a number of years of college. "Adversity," he observed, "seems to be a catalyst for strong bonds."

Emotional problems can be some of the more perplexing and difficult for a couple to deal with. But the commitment to the marriage, providing the spouse who is ill with a known base of support, can be a significant factor in recovery. "We went through a bad time," a wife pointed out, "when our three children were quite young. I was hospitalized for depression. We talked and talked and shared our way back." She feels that her husband was as important as the medical treatment in enabling her to survive and conquer the disorder.

Commitment provides each spouse with the sense of being able to survive all kinds of problems without being emotionally or interpersonally crippled.

ACTION GUIDELINES

Beginning with this chapter, we will draw out some implications for action based on the observations and experiences of our happily-married couples. These action guidelines are consistent with social psychological principles, and should be useful both to those who wish to engage in an enduring, satisfying marriage and to those who are trying to help others pursue that goal.

In this chapter, we have examined the meaning and significance of commitment for an enduring marriage. Commitment means a promise to dedicate oneself to an attachment. Among long-term, happily-married couples, that commitment is both to marriage and to the spouse. Moreover, the commitment is an intense one, as illustrated by their willingness to endure troubled times and to go through the painful process of working out problems. Not everyone is committed to the same degree. Some people, fearing betrayal or disappointment or frustration, may be reluctant to make a firm commitment.

The question here, then, is how can a couple go about deepening their commitment? We should note first of all that the remainder of the book is an answer to the question. That is, commitment is not merely the cause but also the result of a satisfying relationship. Nevertheless, there are some things that can be done to strengthen the commitment.

We noted that commitment is facilitated by a belief in the importance of a stable family life. In other words, commitment is easier to the extent that an individual is convinced of its value. People will commit themselves as they accept the argument that both they and the society in which they live will benefit from their commitment. As Kilpatrick has insisted, "life becomes meaningful mainly through transpersonal commitment," and without that commitment no pursuit of personal growth or liberation will bring meaning.[12] As our couples pointed out, those who are committed reap the benefits of security, support, and survival in a difficult, sometimes treacherous world.

A technique for building or intensifying one's belief in the value of commitment is self-instruction.[13] Most people have used self-instruction at various times to try to manage their behavior. It may take a negative form, as in the case of the man who is tempted to drink excessively and says to himself, "Don't do this. You'll hate yourself in the morning." Or it may take a positive form, as in the case of the woman who doesn't like to run but reminds herself when she longs to stop: "You'll feel so much better about yourself if you stick it out."

Self-instructions are effective for managing various kinds of behavior. In the case of commitment to marrriage, the self-instructions can be used as needed when one is feeling indifferent or troubled or frustrated or angry with one's spouse. For example: "Hang in there, because you'll be far happier in the long run"; "Every marriage has problems; this is just one of those difficult times that you'll have to endure"; and so on. Each individual must find the kind of self-instructions that are effective for himself or herself. The point is that they are one technique for deepening one's commitment.

It is important to note that self-instructions are not a substitute for dealing with problems. For commitment is more than a promise to maintain the marriage. It is a promise to endure and to confront and work through the problems that inevitably come to every couple. Why would someone be unwilling to confront and work through a problem? Why would they be willing, as were our unhappy spouses, to endure an unhappy relationship? For some people, it may seem easier to let the problems continue rather than tolerate the pain of working through them. To confront and work through problems means the individual may have to say things or express feelings or discuss something that he or she prefers to avoid. It may be easier to hope that the problems will go away eventually. There may also be a sense of inadequacy in the face of the problems. The individual may feel that he or she lacks the necessary problem-solving skills. We will discuss the skills used by our couples in chapter 7. They are skills that can be acquired and used by anyone. And they are skills that will be necessary to those who are committed to the spouse and not just to marriage. Both kinds of commitment must be made for a satisfying as well as a long-lasting relationship.

Self-instructions are helpful in strengthening one's own commitment. But it is also possible to strengthen the spouse's commitment through the technique of team building. Businesses are making widespread use of team-building techniques, exercises and activities that increase the solidarity of work groups. One of the outcomes of team building is a greater commitment to the group on the part of the members. One of the ways to gain that commitment is to engage in activities that involve the pursuit of shared goals. For a marriage, this means emphasizing the fact of being a couple who share basic goals in life rather than two individuals who share a house.

A sense of being a couple, of sharing life goals (and, therefore, of building commitment) can be deliberately enhanced by such things as:

1. An exercise in which each one writes down his or her own goals and the goals that he or she believes are held by the spouse. Then the lists are shared and the answers discussed. The spouses understand more fully the goals that each has and they work to create a number of common goals.
2. An attention to language, so that there is an appropriate amount of "we" and "our" as well as "I" and "my." Too much "we" may signal an unhealthy dependence, but too much "I" may signal too few shared goals.
3. Planned, shared activities. One of the primary ways of building commitment is to engage in shared activities that are gratifying to both. We shall discuss this further in chapter 6. Here we want to stress the fact that we live in a society in which "doing your own thing" is a virtue and demands from

careers and families may be heavy. In such a context, the spouses will have to work at being a couple by planning a certain amount of time for activities for themselves.

Once committed, the individual will not likely find it difficult to live with the decision. When we commit ourselves to a course of action we tend to change our attitudes to be consistent with that action. Reservations we had prior to the commitment tend to fade away. Thus, Bart reflected back on the time he got engaged to his wife of three decades:

I didn't want to commit myself at the time. I thought that there were too many uncertainties about my career and the military obligation to think about marriage. But she insisted that I make a decision, and once I did I found that all of my doubts disappeared. In fact, I enthusiastically insisted on the marriage even though my father and some of my relatives thought I was acting rashly.

FOOTNOTES

1. William Kilpatrick, *Identity & Intimacy* (New York: Delta Books, 1975), pp. 232–33.
2. *Ibid.*, p. 43.
3. Daniel Yankelovich, *New Rules: Searching for Self-Fulfillment in a World Turned Upside Down* (New York: Bantam Books, 1981), pp. 247–48.
4. Naomi Quinn, " 'Commitment' in American Marriage: A Cultural Analysis," *American Ethnologist* 9 (November, 1982):775–98.
5. *Ibid.*, p. 793.
6. William L. Roberts, "Significant Elements in the Relationship of Long-Term Married Couples," *International Journal of Aging and Human Development* 10 (no. 3, 1979–80):267.
7. Michael J. Sporakowski and George A. Hughston, "Prescriptions for Happy Marriage: Adjustments and Satisfactions of Couples Married for 50 or More Years," *The Family Coordinator* 27 (October, 1978):321–27.
8. James L. Framo, "Forward," in W. Robert Beavers, *Successful Marriage: A Family Systems Approach to Couples Therapy* (New York: W. W. Norton & Company, 1985) p. vii.
9. Raymond Fleming et al., "Mediating Influences of Social Support on Stress at Three Miles Island," *Journal of Human Stress* 8 (September, 1982):14–22.
10. Reported in *Psychology Today*, December, 1982, pp. 80–81.
11. Robert E. Larzelere and Ted L. Huston, "The Dyadic Trust Scale: Toward Understanding Interpersonal Trust in Close Relationships," *Journal of Marriage and the Family* 42 (1980):595–604.
12. Kilpatrick, *op cit.*, p. 173.
13. Brian T. Yates, *Self-Management* (Belmont, CA.: Wadsworth Publishing Co., 1985), pp. 63–72.

Chapter 5
To Love and To Honor

The French philosopher, Montaigne, warned young people that marriages that are based on physical attraction or sexual desire are most likely to be troubled or to fail. American youth are frequently reminded that they must recognize the inevitable fading of that first flush of passion that surrounds marriage. It all sounds rather bleak. It sounds as though anyone committed to a long-term marriage must come to terms with the early death of the exhilaration and adventure of a new love.

Those in enduring marriages, however, know that the warnings and reminders are only partial truths. Indeed, if a couple has nothing more than sexual attraction to hold them together, their marriage may quickly crumble when the passion that brought them together begins to ebb. But for others, marriage is the parent rather than the dying child of love. President Theodore Roosevelt once noted that the happiest lot of people occurs when lover and sweetheart are not lost in husband and wife. The couples in our research show that it is possible for husband and wife to remain lover and sweetheart. Love doesn't have to die in an enduring marriage. On the contrary, love is able to flower and manifest all of its many-faceted richness in a way not possible outside of a long-term relationship.

THE MEANING AND COURSE OF TRUE LOVE

True love, according to an old song, is a "many-splendored thing." Love is also a many-faceted thing. It has many and varied meanings. We use the word "love" to talk about our feelings for all sorts of things: "I love my mate"; "I love spaghetti and meat balls"; "I loved that movie"; "I love to walk through the park in the mist." And even those who say that they love their mate do not always mean the same thing by it. It is little wonder, then, that poets and song writers have struggled for centuries to express the meaning of love.

Our couples view love as very important, as the foundation of an enduring and satisfying marriage. But they do not confine the meaning of love to that experience that supposedly strikes the individual who "falls in love" of being tossed back and forth between ecstasy and despair. Rather, they see love as a combination of a number of feelings, attitudes, and forms of behavior. Love, according to our respondents, includes four components: sexual feelings, affection and intimacy, liking one's mate, and the selfless kind of love that Erich Fromm wrote about: "the active concern for the life and the growth of that which we love."[1]

Before looking at each of the aspects of love, we should note that Shakespeare was quite right when he observed that the course of true love never did run smooth. The intensity of love varies over time. Our couples all have their ups and downs. The love they feel for each other never stays at one level. None of them married and then lived happily ever after in the glow of intense love. All can talk about the low points in their marriages. But the love never vanishes. It is always there, providing an underlying thread of hope through difficult times and a base for happiness in good times.

The meaning of love, or, more accurately, the kind of love that people need, also varies according to age and sex.[2] As people age, they tend to put less emphasis on sexual intimacy and more on the importance of emotional security and commitment to a satisfying love relationship. At all ages, women tend to place greater emphasis on the importance of emotional security to a satisfying love relationship. Women may be more dependent on the relationship for such things as comfort, support, and security. This is not to say that such things are unimportant for men, for they rate emotional security higher than anything else. They just do not rate it quite as high as women do.

Thus, two of the basic principles of love in an enduring marriage are:

Love involves sexual feelings, affection, intimacy, liking one's mate, and a selfless concern for the mate's well-being.

The intensity of love varies from time to time, and the things that people expect and need in love vary by age and sex.

THE ROLE OF SEX

In chapter 2 we noted the argument of a young woman who said that she doesn't believe that any two people can maintain a strong sexual interest in each other indefinitely. She based her argument on the fact that people need variety. ''Sex gets stale and dull,'' she said, ''if you have the same partner for more than a few years.'' Some young people not only believe that variety is the spice of any sex life, but also that sexuality gradually dies out as people age, particularly in a long-term marriage. If they are right, the prospects for a sexually satisfying long-term marriage are non-existent.

But the notion that sex gradually dies out as people age is a myth. We are not biologically destined to experience radical decline or death of our sexual drive. Americans associate the decline primarily with the diminishing capacity of men. But in some societies, men as old as 90 and even 100 have been known to father children. And men in some parts of India continue to have sex daily when they are 60 years old. Nor is it true that the lack of variety in partners will kill one's sexual desire. Fortunately for those who would like to maintain an active sex life and an enduring marriage as well, there is a good deal of evidence to show that sexual intimacy can occur between two people for many decades. One study of sex among 161 couples who had been married for about 20 years reported that the couples were still experiencing significant pleasure from sexual relations.[3] Seventy percent of the husbands and 57 percent of the wives said that they had great enjoyment from their sex relations in the previous three years. An additional 25 percent of the husbands and 33 percent of the wives reported ''mild pleasure.'' Thus, only 5 percent of the men and 10 percent of the women were indifferent or averse to sex. The frequency of sex relations had dropped. But 14 percent of the couples reported having sex 9 or more times per month during the previous three years.

Even people who have been married for fifty or more years may still have meaningful sex relations. More than half of one group of fifty couples who had been married an average of 55.5 years were still sexually active, or had been within the past five years.[4] One woman told us that the day before her 82-year-old husband went into the hospital for what proved to be a fatal aneurysm, they had had sex. The notions that sex necessarily dies out in old age, or that two people cannot maintain an active sexual interest in each other for a long period of time, are myths.

One of the questions we asked our couples was the extent of agreement between them about sex relations. As Table 5.1 shows, nearly 68 percent of the happily married couples said that they always or almost always agree about sex relations. About 37 percent of those

Table 5.1

Extent of Agreement on Sex Relations

(In Percentages)

	Happy	Mixed	Unhappy
Always Agree	17.2	0	0
Almost Always Agree	50.7	37.1	8.3
Occasionally Disagree	28.7	35.5	30.6
Frequently Disagree	2.4	24.2	36.1
Almost Always Disagree	0.6	1.6	11.1
Always Disagree	0.4	1.6	13.9
	100.0	100.0	100.0

in a marriage where one partner is unhappy, and 8 percent of those in an unhappy marriage, indicated such agreement. We also asked them whether being too tired for sex had been a problem in the past few weeks. Seventy-one percent of the happily married couples, 52 percent of those in a mixed situation, but only 33 percent of the unhappily married said "no" to the question. Thus, the happily married couples are generally satisfied with their sex lives.

For many of the people in happy marriages, however, "satisfied" is too mild a term. For they indicated to us that sex was not merely satisfactory, but a strong and fulfilling part of their marriage. "Our sexual desire in one another is strong, and we are very much in love with each other," said a woman who had been married for nineteen years. A man said that sex with his wife was like "a revival of youth." Another man reported that he and his wife did not have sex as frequently as they would like for various reasons, but when they do have sex "it is a beautiful act of giving and sharing as deeply emotional as it is physical. If either of us felt the other was doing his or her duty, it would spoil the wonder of our lovemaking."

Some of our respondents reported a diminishing of their sex lives, some reported a relatively stable sexual relationship, and some reported an improvement over time. As a woman in the latter category put it:

> My husband and I were friends for a year before we started dating. That was one of the reasons I decided to marry him. We knew that even if the passion died we would still have a friendly relationship. Thank God, the passion hasn't died. In fact, it has gotten more intense. The only thing that has died is the element of doubt or uncertainty that one experiences while dating or in the beginning of a marriage. We are both very affectionate and romantic. Our sexual relationship flows out of this. It is a part of our total life together.

On the other hand, a marriage can be satisfying even with a less than ideal sex life. Slightly over a third of our happily married respondents reported some disagreement with their spouses about sex relations. But differences about sex do not preclude a good marriage. For instance, a number of people told us that they were happy with their marriage even though they did not have sex as frequently as they would like. Generally, males complained of this more than females. But a number of females desired sex more often than their husbands. One husband was well aware of his wife's greater desire and the problems that this had caused:

> Our sex life has usually been beautiful, but I have always been in hard and demanding work, and sometimes, too many times, just too pooped to pop. This frustrates her very much and at times she has been less than forgiving about it.

A lower frequency of sex relations and the disparity between the desires of the husband and wife can be due to a variety of things in addition to being "pooped" from work. Illness can diminish sexual desire. As a result of his wife's heart attack, said a man who had been married for 39 years, she was not as sexually interested as he was. But "I have adjusted to this." People may also get heavily involved in a career or in caring for children, and be too preoccupied as well as too tired for sex. Sometimes family circumstances intervene: "We are very busy and very involved and have a teenager who stays up late, so we don't make love as often as we would like to."

A less-than-ideal sex life does not mean an unhappy marriage. Many couples adjust to the situation in one way or another. Some of our respondents said that their sex lives were irritating or frustrating to them, but insisted that their marriages were still happy ones overall. "There is quite a difference between love and sex," said a woman who had been married for 60 years. Another woman talked about the lack of sex for the past ten years of their 25-year marriage.

> Important to my adjustment to this is that I was once married before where the marriage was almost totally sex and little else. So I suppose a kind of trade-off exists here—I like absolutely everything else about my current marriage. It has not always been this way—perhaps a serious operation he had and perhaps impotence are to blame. If there is another solution, he is not interested in pursuing it.

This woman, incidentally, said that she was "extremely" happy with her marriage overall.

None of our couples, including those who have a strong and fulfilling sexual relationship, identified sex as the most important part of their enduring marriage. Those who have a less-than-ideal sex life, but an otherwise happy marriage, try to deal with the problem by putting sex into perspective. They suggest that they would rather be married to their spouse and have a less-than-ideal sex life than to be married to anyone else and have a better sex life.

> I feel marriages can survive and flourish without today's emphasis on sex. I had a much stronger sex drive than my husband and it was a point of weakness in our marriage. However, it was not so important as friendship, understanding, and respect. That we had lots of, and still do. (married 20 years)

> Our relationship is less physical. This change has decreased satisfaction to a certain degree, but other factors far outweigh this change . . . We seldom look back. We look forward to happy times. (married 32 years)

> We have become more mature in our relationship. At first it seemed to be all physical. Now we have developed a true caring for each other's feelings and interests. The physical part of our relationship is still important, but it takes a back seat to companionship. (married 25 years)

Sex, then, is not the prescription for fulfillment that popular stories and ads make of it. Nor is it, as many believe, one of those cherished possessions of youth that must be enjoyed before it dies away in advancing age. It *is* important, on the other hand, that people agree on their sex lives. That agreement may involve anything from no sex at all to frequent and regular sex relations. A couple may agree to something that is less-than-ideal for one or both of them, or they may find themselves agreeing on a mutual ideal. In any case, it is the agreement rather than anything else that is important. Thus, the principles of sex in a long-term, happy marriage stress both the longevity and a proper perspective on our sex lives:

> *A couple can have an active and fulfilling sex life for most or all of their married lives; neither age nor a continuing relationship kill sex.*

> *A couple can have a satisfying, long-term marriage even though they have a less-than-ideal sex life.*

> *The most important thing about sex is agreement over sexual arrangements and not the kind or frequency of sex relations.*

SHOWING AFFECTION

There is an old story about a man who gave a simple formula for
a long and happy marriage: "I always treated her in a way that
meant she couldn't replace me with a hot-water bottle when I died."
There is wisdom in the folk story, for it emphasizes the importance
of positive action in maintaining a satisfying relationship. And a
part of that positive action, of avoiding the dreary situation of being
replaceable by a hot-water bottle, is showing affection.

There are various ways in which affection can be demonstrated.
They need not be dramatic or innovative. Something as simple as a
smile can be very meaningful: "Sarah has often said that what really
means a lot to her is when I smile at her. *At* her. Not just when I'm
smiling, but when I'm smiling at her because I feel warm towards
her." Physical contact is also a common way to express affection:
"We're touchers, huggers, and kissers;" "I'm a person who needs
to be hugged more than kissed and a grin across the room is good
too. To me this is approval, and I need this."

Our happy couples are fully aware of their need for affection.
They have far fewer problems about demonstration of affection than
do couples in mixed or unhappy marriages (Table 5.2). They have
made a conscious effort to provide each other's needs. As one
woman put it, lots of physical affection was a "mutually agreed on
priority" in her marriage. Such affection, of course, is different
from sexual intimacy. The couple we noted above, who no longer
had sexual relations, still maintained a good deal of physical
intimacy: "We show affection easily, mainly by hugs, cuddling,
and kisses." Ninety-eight percent of our happily-married respondents say they kiss each other every day or almost every day. We
also asked them whether or not showing love had been a problem in
the past few weeks. Eighty-six percent said "no," compared to 67
percent in mixed marriages and 37 percent in unhappy marriages.

In the long run, the expression of affection solidifies the
relationship, enriches the marriage, and bathes the memory in
warmth. As Victor, a school administrator married for 25 years,
explained his feelings to us:

> I was very concerned about my performance as a young man.
> I desperately wanted to do well at my job. I remember little
> about sexual intercourse per se. But I remember at night laying
> in her arms. In that way, she was telling me that I was all right.

That kind of physical sharing was very important. Sex and techniques per se are not that important.

For couples in enduring marriages, then, affection is not something that only occurs when one of the partners desires sex. Rather, sex emerges out of an ongoing relationship of expressed affection. As one woman explained it, she and her husband show a great deal

Table 5.2

Extent of Agreement on Demonstrations of Affection

(In Percentages)

	Happy	Mixed	Unhappy
Always Agree	22.7	0	0
Almost Always Agree	49.2	42.8	13.2
Occasionally Disagree	24.3	39.7	42.1
Frequently Disagree	3.6	15.8	26.3
Almost Always Disagree	0.2	0	15.8
Always Disagree	0	1.6	2.6
	100.0	99.9	100.0

of physical affection, and sex is a natural outcome of this ongoing affection: "I could not turn on sexually on cue if the only time my husband touched me or kissed me was when he wanted sex." Sex is a moment of ecstasy that punctuates our lives; affection is a stream of warm support that enfolds and sustains us. But affection is impotent, of course, unless it is acted out as well as felt:

Affection for your mate must not only be felt but also overtly expressed in some way.

I LIKE YOU

Song writers give us a virtually limitless selection of musical ways to say "I love you" to someone. No one, to our knowledge, has written a song that says "I like you." Yet the couples in our survey clearly indicate that liking one's mate is more fundamental than loving one's mate. "I like Frank so much," said a woman who has been married for 35 years. "The like was probably more important than the passionate love." Many of our respondents pointed out that their love developed as a result of their friendship and their liking for each other. And they agree that it is the liking that is the glue of their relationship. A teacher, married 22 years, said: "Yes, I really love my husband. But it was the liking that helped us get through the times I wanted to wring his neck."

We asked people to what extent they agreed with the statement, "I like my mate as a person." Among the happily married, 98.2 percent agreed, while the remaining 1.8 percent said they were "neutral." Not a single one of the respondents in happy marriages disagreed with it. Those in mixed and unhappy unions were far less likely to strongly agree with the statement (Table 5.3).

People in happy marriages do not minimize the importance of the other aspects of love. Rather, they stress the point that liking is a fundamental and essential part of loving. You can, of course, like someone without developing a full love for that person. But you can't create an enduring love when you do not have a basic liking for the person. Miriam, who rated herself as "extremely happy" in her marriage, underscored the importance of liking in an enduring relationship:

I feel liking a person in marriage is as important as loving that person. I have to like him so I will love him when things aren't

Table 5.3

Percent of Responses to: "I Like My Mate as a Person"

	Happy	Mixed	Unhappy
Strongly Agree	70.7	27.4	13.2
Agree	27.6	53.2	44.7
Neutral	1.8	17.7	31.6
Disagree	0	1.6	7.9
Strongly Disagree	0	0	2.6
	100.1	99.9	100.0

so rosy. Friends enjoy each others company—enjoy doing things together. This is important to an enduring marriage. We spend an unusually large amount of time together. We work at the same institution—offices just a few feet apart. But we still have things to do and say to each other on a positive note after being together through the day. That's why friendship really ranks high in my reasons for our happy marriage.

Our couples suggested a number of ways in which liking one's mate benefits a relationship. In addition to being a necessary foundation for love, those who like their mates will enjoy the time they have together. This may sound like a superfluous statement, but there are couples who appear to be either uneasy or unhappy in each other's presence. As we noted in our discussion of those who have long-term, unsatisfying marriages, some couples remain in a bland relationship and some in a "who's afraid of Virginia Woolf" relationship for decades.

In the first flush of a new relationship, it may be the overwhelming sensation of romantic love that causes a person to want to be with his or her beloved all the time. But in the long run, it is the liking that leads people to want to spend their time together. A woman who rated herself as "extremely happy" in her marriage, said: "We enjoy being together and I still don't know anyone that I like better than my husband." Similarly, a man who has been happily married for 34 years, told us: "My wife is delightful. I like to be with her. Her aim is to make me very happy. My aim is to make her happy." And another man who rated his marriage as extremely happy, reported: "Jen is just the best friend I have. I would rather spend time with her, talk with her, be with her than anyone else. If I didn't like her, I couldn't stay married regardless of my other beliefs."

A long-term marriage means a lot of hours spent together. Some people doubt that any two individuals can truly enjoy each other's company, and find each other stimulating and interesting, for decades. Our couples put the doubt to rest. It is not only possible, but it happens among those who genuinely like each other.

Another benefit of liking one's mate is that it helps people get through the inevitable hard times of a marriage. Liking your mate, our couples say, makes it easier to overcome problems and disagreements. It is the principle of being able to overlook things, to forgive, and to be tolerant of those we regard as our good friends. Lois regards her liking for her husband as the most important factor in her nineteen-year marriage:

> I have always respected and admired Jim's qualities of sense of humor, kindness, and generosity since we first met. As time has gone by and our marriage has had its ups and downs, these qualities have kept our marriage going. As with any good friendship, we trust each other to always be there through thick and thin and like each other so that we are tolerant of each other's failings and can solve any differences.

Similarly, one husband told us that he could have given a whole
range of different responses to the various questions, depending
upon when in his marriage the questions had been asked. But "most
of the questions are really unimportant no matter what way they are
answered if you really care for and like the person you married."

One other benefit of liking one's mate is the gratification that it
brings both to the marriage and to each spouse's life in general.
"Living with someone you really like as a person," said one wife,
"is a joy." To like one's mate is to add an element of joy to life in
general as well as to the marriage. As we noted in the second
chapter, Americans depend upon their marriages to help them attain
a fulfilling life. Those who like their mates have a relationship at the
core of their being that gives them a source of richness and stability
upon which they can draw in dealing with other matters. Judith,
married for 31 years, stressed this point:

> I *like* my husband. Having confidence in one another, sharing
> laughter, and knowing that we think alike, our aspirations for
> the future have every possibility of coming to pass. He is my
> rock, my base, cheering me on in whatever I do.

Love covers a multitude of sins, according to the Bible. "Like,"
we find, covers a multitude of marital sins. Our couples insist that
it is the foundation of love, the basis for a happy and meaningful
relationship, and a tool for effective problem-solving. When you
like your mate as a person, as one wife put it, you change the "job"
of marriage into the "pleasure" of marriage. And you have a
chance to build the fulfilling kind of relationship described by Mary,
who spoke of her feelings about her "strong, caring, and loving
mate" of thirty years:

> I really don't know what is his strongest feature—his loving
> care of us or the beauty he sees in everything. No matter what
> happens, as long as I have him, the sun will rise tomorrow.

But what is it that people like about their spouse? Happily
married people tend to say that their mates get more interesting to
them over time and that they find satisfaction in the achievements of
their mates. They see their mates, in other words, as individuals
who are growing and who are engaged with life. In addition, over
and again, our respondents indicated that the things that they really

liked in their spouses were qualities of caring, giving, integrity, and a sense of humor. Some mentioned various other qualities, such as intelligence, achievements, and optimism. But caring, giving, integrity, and a sense of humor were the qualities most often mentioned. For example:

> I have found in my mate a growing and exciting friendship. She is closer to me than any person has ever been. It is good because we can laugh together. I like my mate for many reasons. First, because she is a kind and compassionate person. She is genuinely concerned about people and their needs. She has an honest, forthright outlook on life.

Of course, there have been works of fiction that describe the anguished life of a man or woman who loves and cleaves to someone who is thoroughly unlikeable. Whether that ever actually happens is not a matter of debate. But the people in our survey define their mates as likeable people. In essence, they are saying very similar things about their mates: I am married to someone who cares about me, who is concerned for my well-being, who gives as much or more than he or she gets, who is open and trustworthy, and who is not mired down in a somber, bleak outlook on life. Fictional characters may embark on a quest of love to redeem an obnoxious individual and transform that individual by the power of their selfless love, but the happily-married people in our sample express no such sense of mission. Rather, they express feelings of gratitude and relief that they have married someone who is basically an appealing, likeable individual.

Is love, like justice, blind in this? Are they seeing their mates through the distorted eyes of love? No doubt their evaluations are colored by their commitment and love. But they are not blind. They know the deficiencies of their mates. They all acknowledge the rough times of their marriages, and they have all had those rough times. And they know about the flaws in their mates. In fact, it is very important to recognize the flaws, for one of the things that people in long-term, happy marriages do, as we shall discuss in a later chapter, is educate each other on becoming more likeable individuals.

But they also know the likeable qualities that are even more important than the deficiencies and the difficulties they have encountered. And they seem to have that quality of looking primarily at the likeable rather than the undesirable characteristics of their mates. They have what we call a perspective of positive selection. We all select certain things to focus on when we observe anyone or anything. Two people can look at the same thing, but focus on very different aspects. One person may look at a flower garden and find it hard to enjoy the flowers because he sees a few weeds. Another looks at the same garden, passes quickly over the weeds, and exults in the beauty of the flowers. The people in our sample are like the latter individual. They are not ignorant of the deficiencies of their mates, but they choose to focus on the likeable qualities. As one husband put it:

> When I married I figured it was for life. I knew my wife-to-be, and liked what I knew. She is not perfect, but her weak points to me, which are very few, I don't worry about. Her strong points overcome them too much. I'm not perfect, and I believe she sees me in the same light.

Moreover, the people in our sample see their mates as the kind of individuals who are likeable in general, not just likeable as a spouse. Frank, married 34 years, spoke of both his own feelings for his wife and also the reaction of others:

> We are more than husband and wife. We are lovers. After all the years of hard times and now the comfortable, secure times, we still place each other first in importance. As a person, I can't think of anyone who doesn't like her. She's such a radiant, friendly, unselfish person. I have been surprised and proud of the many traits, skills, and accomplishments of this woman.

And a wife made a similar point about her husband, who is the kind of person anyone would like:

> Don is a kind and generous person. He gives me a lot of freedom to grow. He is a person I would like to know even if we weren't married. He has all the attributes I value in another person.

Liking, then, is so important that we might be well served by a new generation of song-writers who would extol its many-splendored nature. The principles of liking are fundamental to an enduring marriage:

It is critically important to like your mate as a person, more important than to feel passionate love.

Liking your mate as a person greatly facilitates working through the problems of both marriage and life.

Those who like their mates as persons see their mates as individuals who are caring, giving, honest, and who possess a sense of humor.

THE HEART OF LOVE

Love includes sexual attraction, expressed affection, and a fundamental liking of one's mate as a person. And at the heart of love is that focus on the other that psychoanalyst Erich Fromm talked about—a concern for the life and growth of one's beloved. A marriage counselor told us that at some point in his counseling he always asks each member of a couple who comes to him, "What can *you* do to improve this relationship?" The question is usually unexpected, for most people have clearly in mind what their mates could do to improve the situation but they have given little or no thought to what they themselves could do.

Our couples appear to have escaped the trap of "me-ism," that affliction that many observers say is the bane of American society today. We have become a narcissistic people, according to some critics. We are infatuated with our individual needs and obsessed with the quest for self-knowledge and self-fulfillment.[5] The extent to which the American people have become narcissistic is arguable. In any case, the people in our sample give no evidence of being caught up in that pattern of life. They recognize the importance of focusing on the needs of their mates as well as on their own needs. One husband said that an important attitude necessary to make a marriage work is "complete consideration for your partner's happiness and well-being. If this attitude is maintained by both parties, there would be no divorce." Another said that a successful marriage demands that you "*give* sixty percent of the time. You have to put more in than you take out." And a woman, very happy in her twenty-six year marriage, said that the most important thing in her relationship with her husband is love. She defined love as "the concern for the other that allows you to open up to each other, to accept, to forgive, to smooth, to understand, and to enjoy fully."

Our respondents not only recognize a need for both husband and wife to focus on each other's needs, but also perceive their own mates as doing just that. Over and over again, they told us, not just what they are doing to fulfill the needs of their mates, but what their mates are doing to fulfill their needs. They see their mates as individuals who are giving as much or more to the marriage as they are getting from it. They seem impressed by the fact that their mates genuinely care about them. "My marriage is enduring," said one man, "because my wife has given me a safe haven in which to live, receive care and affection, and grow along with her. We each have the best interests of each other at heart." A woman put the matter succinctly: "He still treats me as though he loves me."

How does one express concern for the well-being of the other? How does that selfless kind of love express itself in the warp and woof of everyday living? Our respondents gave a number of specifics. Some of them pointed out that their spouses tried to do things to make them happy or to please them. This can mean as many different things as there are diverse needs among people, but it always means being sensitive to the needs of your mate. This sensitivity covers everything from fundamental needs ("he gives me space to grow," said a wife with gratitude) to specific incidents ("once when I felt very down about a career failure," said a husband, "she wrote me a little note reminding me that she loved me as much as ever"). People in long-term, happy marriages are not so immersed in themselves that they are unable to be sensitive to the needs of their mates. On the contrary, they are able to focus as much on their spouses' as their own needs and happiness.

Another way that love is manifest in everyday life is respect. Our respondents feel that they both give and receive respect. They define respect as a regard for the worth and the rights of the other. A part of respect is the willingness to accept the other as he or she is. After two decades of marriage, Judy still calls her husband her "lover," and says of their relationship:

I can tell him anything and he listens. He does not criticize me and does not try to change me. When we married we both accepted each other the way we were. If we offer advice to each other, it is politely and respectfully given. We both realize that we are trying, and don't come down very hard on each other.

Respect is also evident in anything that affirms the dignity of the other. Thus, one couple said that they never used derogatory words about each other. And a woman said that her husband treated her as "an intelligent human being," something which is significant to that half of the human race that has too frequently been defined as mentally inferior.

Finally, love means having someone you can trust. If your mate is actively trying to fulfill your needs, it means you can always rely on him or her. A man who has been married for 61 years said that his marriage meant that "there was always someone to rely on, and if you were ill, there was always someone who really cared about you. And gave you encouragement when things went wrong. And stood by you." And a wife noted that one of the most important things in her marriage was the fact that she and her husband could solve problems together: "Underlying this is a sense of unconditional love. No matter what I say or do, I will be loved." Thus, love for our respondents means, among other things, security. They have emotional security because they have someone who is there to listen, to support, to help.

Love manifests itself in efforts to make the other happy, in respect for the dignity of the other, and in being a source of emotional security for the other.

ACTION GUIDELINES

Love in a long-term, enduring marriage is a complex set of attitudes, feelings, and behavior. It is important to recognize that the behavior does not depend upon certain feelings or attitudes. That is, people can continue to try to make their spouses happy, to show respect, and to be a source of security even though they may not feel passion or even affection. One of the interesting things about behaving in a certain way is that it tends to create the appropriate attitudes and feelings. Continuing to behave in a loving way toward one's mate, therefore, can renew the positive feelings. It is normal for people's feelings about their mates to vary over time. Indeed, if couples broke up when their feelings about each other were negative, the divorce rate would be near 100 percent.

"I can't help the way I feel," is a common saying. But people can help the way they behave, and if they behave in a loving way they are likely to find their feelings changing in a loving direction as well. This is a sound social psychological principle that comes out of cognitive dissonance studies. If we change our behavior we will find our attitudes and feelings changing to be consistent with the behavior. As a psychiatrist has phrased it: "Since we are what we do, if we want to change what we are we must begin by changing what we do, must undertake a new mode of action."[6] Perceptive people have discovered the principle for themselves. A wise friend once told us: "Is there anyone you don't like? Do something nice for that person. You can't keep doing nice things for someone and continue to dislike them." Our respondents seem to know the importance of behaving in a loving way independently of how they are feeling at any particular time.

It is important also for people to recognize individual differences, and differences over time, in what their spouses need. In the play, *My Fair Lady*, Henry Higgins sings a song that asks why a woman can't be more like a man. He is perplexed by the fact that women don't respond to things as he does. But those in enduring marriages do not ask their mates, why can't you be like me? Nor do they ask each other why they can't be like most other men and women. They accept each other for what they are and love them into being what they can become. To create a happy, long-term marriage, people need to be sensitive to their mate's needs, and attempt to fulfill those needs even though they may be different from theirs or from those that they regard as typical of others.

A couple's sexual life will change over time. But most couples can have an active and fulfilling sex life throughout their marriage. People can also have an enduring and satisfying marriage with a less-than-ideal sex life. Sex, therefore, must be kept in perspective. Many people have been misled by the *Playboy* mentality that exalts sex into the focal point of life and that portrays sex as an invariably exquisite experience. Some couples have tried swinging in an effort to rekindle a sexual richness in their lives. But swinging tends to disillusion and disrupt people rather than enrich them. The promise of sexual utopia is realized only on the pages of slick magazines. In real life, people must work at their sexual relationship. Many report that their sexual lives become more rather than less satisfying over time. Those in enduring marriages who fall short of that say that the other aspects of the relationship far outweigh in importance the sexual part of their lives. In either case, sex is not regarded as the most fundamental part of their satisfaction. It is important, but it is not crucial. Those who wish to build a long-term, satisfying relationship will work at a mutually acceptable sexual life rather than at any "ideal" portrayed in the popular literature.

More important than sex is affection. And it is important to overtly express affection. Husbands, in particular, need to attend to such expressions at times other than when they want to have sex, for men are particularly prone to neglect this important dimension of a relationship. A wife who has been happily married for 40 years recalled that one of the things that enriched her life was her husband telling her every day that he loved her. Looks, words, caresses, and actions—they are all ways of expressing affection toward another. There is an old story about a reticent Vermonter who once confided to a friend: "I love Martha so much, it's all I can do to keep from telling her about it." Some people are reticent in general, and or some feel awkward about expressing affection openly, but those who desire an enduring and satisfying marriage will find it imperative to cultivate the habit of expressing affection.

We stressed the critical importance of liking one's mate as a person. There are two ways in which people can act on this principle. First, they can strive to make themselves more likeable people, keeping in mind that the qualities that people like in others include caring, giving, honesty, and a sense of humor. In addition, they need to be sensitive to the particular other things that their mates like in people and try to develop such qualities. Second, people can help their mates become more likeable individuals. As we shall discuss in chapter 8, one of the things that people in enduring marriages do is to educate each other. The people in our sample frequently told us of ways in which their mates had helped them to change, either to develop certain desirable qualities or to get rid of certain undesirable ones.

One method of enhancing mutual liking is for each spouse to write down on a piece of paper what he or she likes generally about people of the opposite sex, what he or she likes about the spouse, and what he or she thinks the spouse likes about him or her. These lists are exchanged and discussed. It is an interesting exercise to see how much one's perceptions square with those of one's spouse and to be reminded of the kinds of things that are important to each of the partners.

Finally, the heart of love is a concern for the well-being, and an active effort to fulfill the needs, of one's mate. Responding to this principle may involve asking oneself various questions. What can I do today to enhance the happiness of my mate? What can I do to show that I respect him or her? In some cases, that may mean that the individual must *stop* doing something. For example, one man had developed the habit of joking in public about his wife's lack of intelligence. He didn't really believe what he was saying; it had just become a pattern among their group of friends. One day she gently pointed out that such "kidding" was quite demeaning: "I told him that I knew he didn't really feel that way about me, but that I was still embarrassed and a little hurt when he said such things in front of our friends." She helped her husband by educating him to be more thoughtful. He loved her by stopping something that detracted from her well-being.

The case above illustrates what is perhaps a major problem, namely that we tend to take each other for granted, and to respond mainly when our spouses clearly indicate a special need. But this kind of love should be an ongoing pattern. And that means people may have to consciously plan it. We know a corporate manager who keeps a piece of paper in his desk upon which he has written the words: "Give strokes." He is aware of the importance of praising his workers, and reminds himself daily to do so when it is warranted. Some people in enduring marriages seem to have a mental piece of paper that reminds them to continue to focus on the needs and well-being of their spouses. Others need to consciously remind themselves from time to time, perhaps even to carry a piece of paper around that reminds them. Whatever the method, it is important for spouses to continue to give each other strokes, affection, support, and whatever else each of them needs day by day.

Again, we must emphasize that this does not mean total selflessness. Absorption in either one's own interests or in the interests of one's spouse will let the relationship quietly slip into a pattern of dead ritualism. People can follow the advice of one school of thought today and put the emphasis on themselves and their own needs. Or they can follow the opposite course and sacrifice themselves in behalf of someone else. Neither course of action is conducive to a happy relationship. No one should be a doormat for others. Neither is it healthy for people to become so absorbed in their own needs that their lives become a kind of navel contemplation. Self-absorption can only mean other-neglect. And marriages can survive the agony of crises easier than the slow erosion of indifference or neglect. Our respondents repeatedly emphasized the importance of being neither a doormat nor a navel contemplator. The focus must not be "I" or "you," but "we." That, to them, is the meaning of love.

FOOTNOTES

1. Erich Fromm, *The Art of Loving* (New York: Bantam Books, 1956), p. 22.
2. Mararet Neiswender Reedy, James E. Birren and K. Warner Schaie, "Age and Sex Differences in Satisfying Love Relationships Across the Adult Life Span," *Human Development* 24 (1981):52–66.
3. Ben N. Ard, Jr., "Sex In Lasting Marriages: A Longitudinal Study," *The Journal of Sex Research* 13 (1977):274–85.
4. William L. Roberts, "Significant Elements in the Relationship of Long-Married Couples," *International Journal of Aging and Human Development* 10 (1979–80):269.
5. Christopher Lasch, *The Culture of Narcissism* (New York: Warner Books, 1979).
6. Allen Wheelis, *How People Change* (New York: Harper & Row, 1973), p. 101.

Chapter 6
The Two Become One:
Dilemma or Opportunity?

Leo Tolstoy wrote of one of his fictional characters that the man was so enamored of his new wife that "he did not know where he ended and she began." A different view of the married life was presented by Oscar Wilde, who had one of his characters say that the charm of married life was that it made "a life of deception absolutely necessary" for both the man and the woman. Tolstoy's character expresses the long-standing idea that in marriage a man and a woman become "one flesh," that their individual identities merge into a new entity. Wilde's character, on the other hand, implied that marriage not only fails to unite two people, but adds a flaw to their personalities as they struggle to maintain their individuality.

Marriage counselors take a middle road between the two positions. They accept neither the merging nor the life of deception as a desirable life style. They stress the need for a husband and wife to maintain their own identities and pursue some of their individual interests while sharing some part of their lives. But that poses a dilemma. How does a couple both become one flesh and retain their individuality? How can people successfully walk the precarious line between the two without becoming so merged that they lose their individuality or working so hard to retain their individuality that they are not truly a couple? To answer the question, we must first look at the patterns of communication and consensus that exist among our long-term, happily-married couples.

COMMUNICATION PATTERNS

It has become a truism to laud the importance of communication in marriage. We would point out, however, that the notion that communication is a panacea for marital problems is a myth. We spoke once with a woman who insisted that all of the problems of the world were problems of communication. "If only people would communicate with each other," she argued, "they could resolve any differences." "But what if," we asked her, "two people communicated effectively and learned thereby that they don't really like each other? What if they each learn that the other has beliefs or behavior that the one regards as abhorrent?" Communication will not solve every problem. In a marriage, even if the communication is clear, the spouses may find that they can do no more than recognize that they cannot agree on a particular issue.

Ironically, while effective communication will not guarantee a successful marriage, a successful marriage requires effective communication. A great deal of research on marital satisfaction underscores the importance of communication. The more that people talk together, the more likely they are to be satisfied with their marriages.[1] In fact, Howard Markman reported a longitudinal study of 26 couples who were planning to be married.[2] He measured the couples' perceptions of their communication patterns at the time and three subsequent times over a five-year period. He found that the more positively the couples rated their communication prior to getting married, the more satisfied they were with their marriages after 5 years. Couples with poorer communication patterns initially were more likely to encounter serious problems with the union. In a survey of marriage counselors the trouble area most frequently named as a cause of marital dissolution was breakdown in communication.[3]

The importance of communication is dramatically illustrated by Jenny's account of the course of her 15-year, unhappy marriage. She was twenty-two, and her husband, Phil, was thirty when they were married. Both were introspective kinds of people. She was a nurse and he was a psychologist. She recalls being a lonely child who "rarely, if ever, confided totally in another." Phil's childhood was difficult. Each of them, therefore, was insecure. But they handled the insecurity differently. Jenny was "fearful, tearful and depressed." Phil handled his insecurity by denying that he had any. Jenny discussed what happened in a third-person account:

> So we have two people who did not communicate or prepare themselves adequately with each other before marriage. They did not discuss important things like potential problems; things they liked and didn't like about each other; what they wanted for themselves and from the marriage; and the balance of

power (and much of their later trouble was a power struggle, a problem further compounded by the fact that neither could or would admit to this). They argued, discussed and reached unresolved impasses on many things—in-laws, finances, children—but they never talked about the real issues—their own fears and vulnerabilities. This contributed to the final breakup of their marriage within two months of their 15th anniversary. And they never even discussed the breakup. Not the reasons for it or anything. Not how they felt. They just slid into it as they had into marriage and through 15 years of marriage.

Communication will not resolve all marital problems, but effective communication is essential for an enduring and satisfying marriage.

Communicate What?

What Jenny's experience underscores is the need for *effective* communication, which means communication about things that are really important to the spouses as well as so-called "small talk." There is a direct relationship between marital satisfaction and self-disclosure. People who have happy marriages talk about their marriage, their families, love, sex, their emotions and feelings, finances, and all other matters that are of concern to them.[4] A study of 50 couples who had been married an average of 55.5 years reported that the spouses confided in each other in virtually all matters.[5]

Of course, effective communication does not occur merely because people are talking. Communication, we should keep in mind, goes on continually. As someone has put it, you cannot *not* communicate. The so-called silent treatment is a rather strong mode of communicating anger and displeasure. Those who do not share their thoughts or feelings with others will find that the others attribute thoughts and feelings to them on the basis of their behavior and their nonverbal cues. They are communicating, but they are not communicating effectively. On the other hand, those who talk but do not talk about the things that matter deeply or that bother them will also not communicate effectively. Jenny and Phil talked about a lot of things. They argued about a lot of things. But in retrospect Jenny realizes that they never talked about the things that were really bothering them. They never communicated about the things that were most important to each of them. In contrast, couples who have long-term, satisfying marriages have learned to communicate effectively, which involves a discussion of matters that each spouse regards as important as well as talking about minor matters. Our respondents indicated that they talk about both major and minor matters. They value having someone with whom they can share all of their thoughts and feelings and concerns. When asked how often they calmly discuss something, 62 percent of the happy couples said one or more times every day; only 36 percent of those in mixed and 21 percent in unhappy marriages reported such frequency. Often, the discussion is more than calm; it is lively, intellectually interesting, or emotionally stirring. Twenty-eight percent said that they have a stimulating exchange of ideas with their spouse at least daily, and another 66 percent said that they have such an exchange at least once a month or more.

We should note that although our couples stressed the importance of freely talking with each other about *anything*, they did not say that they fully disclosed *everything* to each other. Some marriage counselors and some workshop leaders have urged couples to be totally honest and open with each other, to reveal exactly how each is feeling and thinking. But while it may be useful to fully disclose one's feeling to a counselor or a therapist, it can be very damaging to do so to one's mate. Our respondents indicated a sensitivity to this issue. They do not necessarily share whatever they are feeling or thinking with each other. They are sensitive to the impact that such sharing will have on the other. "There have been times," said Bill, happily married for over thirty years, "when I have not told her about some of my feelings, because I knew it would hurt her and I knew the feeling would pass." A wife pointed out that she withheld some of her thoughts and feelings because she would "never do or say anything that might hurt Gary or harm our relationship." Indeed, there is some research that shows that too much as well as too little self-disclosure can damage a relationship.[6] Our couples recognize this, and make the important distinction between anything and everything.

Happy couples have regular, frequent communication about all matters of concern and interest, but they do not engage in total self-disclosure.

The Language of Communication

Effective communication occurs both verbally and nonverbally among happy couples. Words are sometimes unnecessary, even for experiences of intense intimacy. Midge, a writer who has been married for over two decades, told us that she and her husband had serious problems with a son for a number of years. They became emotionally and physically exhausted in dealing with the problems, and their exhaustion strained their own relationship. They came to the edge of marital breakdown. But they refused to give up, eventually worked through the problems with the son, and saw him change into a responsible young adult. Their own relationship improved dramatically. And one of the most intimate moments of their marriage, she said, was the day they went to the airport to watch their son take off to a meaningful career. As the plane left, they looked at each other. They said nothing. But in the look they shared again all the days of pain and the exultation of overcoming. It was wordless but intense. It was a shared moment of intimacy that remains as a peak experience in their memories.

One of the interesting aspects of communication is the special language that virtually all couples develop. This special language, what we call couple argot, is both verbal and nonverbal. It enables couples to communicate meaningfully with each other while excluding others. Couple argot is the use of words and gestures that have peculiar meaning to the couple. One couple indicated that they had a particular phrase at parties that was a signal that one of them wished to leave. Another said that they signaled each other when they desired sexual relations by wetting a finger, putting it on an arm, and making a sizzling sound as though the arm was extremely hot. Couples may also make up words, or use words that their children made up or mispronounced when they were learning to talk, or even use a foreign language that those around them do not understand. A woman told us how her parents, who have been married over 40 years, use foreign languages as their couple argot:

My parents grew up on the lower East side of New York City. They spoke Russian, Polish, and Ukranian as well as English. To this day, they will switch to another language if they don't want to be understood and wish to say something privately. Sometimes it is just a funny story that someone has told my Dad and he will relate it to Mom and she'll burst out laughing. They have a separate world of communication in their marriage.

There is a latent function to couple argot. In addition to enabling the couple to communicate exclusively with each other, it contributes to a shared history of intimacy. In chapter 2, we discussed the need for intimacy and the role of marriage in providing that intimacy. Couple argot helps develop intimacy because it emphasizes the separation of the couple from all others and the binding of the couple into a unique entity. Each time a particular word or gesture is used, it reminds each of the spouses of a history of experiences. And each time the word or gesture is used it is a reaffirmation of commitment to the marriage.

Both verbal, including couple argot, and nonverbal modes of communication are important to the development of intimacy.

Learning to Communicate

For some people, communication occurs easily because they grew up in homes where they learned to communicate effectively. Their family life was marked by a rich and open pattern of communication. Meal times were times of discussion. Private chats with mother or father occurred easily. Others, however, grew up in homes with more reserved and reticent atmospheres. Meal times were more quiet. Conversation was limited to the necessities. For them, communication is more problematic.

Those couples who communicate effectively prior to marriage have, as we noted, a decided advantage. But all couples can learn to communicate more effectively over time. Communication skills can be developed. Our respondents underscored the possibilities for learning in their reflections on their communication. Some did insist that they had *never* made any major decisions without discussing them with each other. Some said that they always communicated well. Anne, extremely happy in her 32-year marriage, said: "We have always confided in each other and talked things through, whether vacation plans, money plans, or child-raising questions."

Others, however, noted that their communication skills had to be developed. "I don't think we understood each other until we were in our thirties," one husband remarked. That was ten years after they were married. It was then, he said, that they stopped playing games with each other and started really talking. In some cases, painful events were the stimulus to better communication. A wife of 38 years noted that she and her husband had always discussed major decisions after a problem occurred in the first year of their marriage. Her husband had bought their first car without consulting her. The car broke down. The husband sold it at a loss, but then only got half of the sale price because the buyer skipped town. Since that traumatic experience, they have discussed all of their decisions. Some couples have learned to communicate through marriage encounter groups or through the help of a therapist. George, a businessman married for 29 years, said that a therapist helped him learn to express his feelings:

> I always had a problem telling my wife just how I felt. I still have a problem, but I'm much better. My therapist helped me see that my mother and father never encouraged me to share any feelings. That's why it's so tough for me to do it. I have to actually tell myself to express my feelings even now.

Spouses, of course, help each other to develop communication skills. George pointed out that his wife helped him by urging him periodically to be honest about his feelings. Mutual encouragement (or what, in chapter 8, we call mutual education) may be necessary for a couple to enhance their skills. But a number of other factors are also important. For one thing, when an individual opens up to another individual, there is always a certain risk involved. Some people may not open up because they are ashamed for anyone to know just how they feel, or because they fear that the other will rebuke them or despise them or simply think less of them because of the way they feel. Thus, if they are going to engage in self-disclosure, they must have someone that they can trust. Without a climate of trust, there can be no effective communication. "You have to be able to talk to your partner," said Sheila, a secretary married for 25 years. "When the line of communication is stopped, the chances for your marriage are small." But Sheila is well aware of the risks of communication: "Your partner has to be someone that you can trust with anything from the material things to your inner feelings. He has to be someone you can trust." Happy couples create the climate of trust in which they can each share with the other without the risk of deprecation or rebuke.

There is another important aspect to the climate of trust—it is the assurance that the other is listening. Our respondents said that it is important to be able to disclose oneself with impunity and also to be confident that the other person is actively listening, seriously trying to understand what is being said. As a wife of 31 years put it: "The most important one ingredient in our marriage is communication—open, honest, real communication. Talk, then talk some more. And listen and really hear!"

Communication specialists have amply stressed the importance of listening. What is sometimes not stressed, however, are the risks and costs of listening. It requires a good deal of energy to listen effectively. The listener must be sensitive to non-verbal as well as verbal cues. The listener must focus on the other person and not be distracted or allow his or her mind to wander when the speaker has said something that reminds the listener of another train of thought. The listener must run the risk of having the speaker's message affect the way the listener feels about the speaker. Some people may not want to know about the fears and frustrations of their spouses because they like to think of their spouses as flawless characters, or they may be unwilling to acknowledge that their relationship is anything other than deeply satisfying. But the alternatives to listening may be even less acceptable. A woman married for 46 years said: "Phillip is sometimes reluctant to listen to me, but he has learned that it is better for me to find someone else who will listen." A climate of trust means that each spouse can depend upon the other to accept the risks and the costs of both self-disclosure and active listening.

> *Communication skills can be developed in the course of marriage through mutual encouragement and a climate of trust that allows the partners to accept the risks and costs of both self-disclosure and listening.*

CONSENSUS PATTERNS

The discussion of communication patterns showed that couples in long-term, happy marriages do not totally merge with each other. They do not believe in total self-disclosure. On the other hand, they do disclose more with each other than they do with anyone else. We will see something of the same outcome in consensus patterns. There is a striking amount of agreement. But there is also some disagreement. In essence, the couples tend to agree on the things that they define as of fundamental importance and tolerate areas of disagreement on other matters. Thus, 84.4 percent of the happy couples felt that they always or almost always agreed on aims and goals and those things they believed important (Table 6.1). As one husband put it: "I think the success of our marriage is due in large part to having many common values and that we agree on basically most things that are important in our lives together. This is particularly true for issues related to careers, money, and family lifestyle."

Table 6.1

Extent of Agreement on Aims, Goals, and Things Believed Important

	Happy	Mixed	Unhappy
Always Agree	28.3	12.5	5.3
Almost Always Agree	56.1	51.6	28.9
Occasionally Disagree	13.2	23.4	34.2
Frequently Disagree	2.2	10.9	13.2
Almost Always Disagree	0.2	1.6	15.8
Always Disagree	0	0	2.6
	100.0	100.0	100.0

Interests, Activities, and Friends

Two-thirds of our happy respondents said they always or almost always agree about the matter of leisure time interests and activities, and three-fourths said they always or almost always agree about friends. To keep those figures in perspective, we should note that from one-fourth to one-third of the respondents perceive some degree of disagreement about interests, activities, or friends. Disagreement in such areas does not mean that an individual cannot have a satisfying marriage. Healthy couples know how to tolerate differences as well as enjoy consensus.

Some degree of consensus on interests, activities, and friends is important, however, if husband and wife are to continue to be best friends. A problem may occur in some marriages at the so-called empty-nest stage if the partners have not maintained a set of shared interests and activities. One woman told us that her husband suddenly became a workaholic when their children were grown. He had little time for her, and she was becoming increasingly bored and unhappy. The husband's ''sudden'' passion for work was really a reflection of the fact that they had not cultivated their own relationship during the years their children were growing up. They were not really a couple; they were two parents who shared the same home in which they were rearing their children. In contrast, Betty, who defined herself as very happy in her 25-year marriage, told us:

> We enjoy doing things together. We have always kept time to do things as a couple even when we had small children. We realized we would not always have them at home, so we maintained our relationship.

For long-term satisfaction, it is important to maintain the sense of being a couple, even if one of the partners occasionally has to do something that he or she finds less than interesting. Another wife said that people have to enjoy doing things together ''like fishing and playing volleyball with friends. If there's something you don't enjoy doing and your mate does, go ahead and do it once in awhile because he enjoys it.'' A number of spouses told us that they did some things with their mates that they would not do alone because they knew that the activity gave pleasure to their mates. Even though the activity was not one that they would have chosen, they got enjoyment from it simply because they knew that their mates were having a good time. Satisfaction is maximized if the activities are inherently enjoyed by both husband and wife. But an occasional activity which is primarily of interest to only one of the spouses may be an important way to maintain a sense of being a couple rather than merely two individuals who happen to share a house.

Consensus about activities, interests, and friends enhances marital satisfaction and helps maintain the sense of being a couple.

Life Around the Home

Our couples also perceive a good deal of consensus with regard to various aspects of life at home, including the decision-making process and various aspects of their relationships. We noted in the last chapter that there are striking differences in the extent of consensus over sexual relationships between the happy, mixed, and unhappy couples. Over two-thirds of the happy couples perceive agreement on sexual matters. The happy couples also indicate that it is important to agree on matters about the children and a variety of other aspects of family life.

Thus, there is a good deal of consensus about everyday matters. In his study of 50 couples who had been married at least 50 years, William Roberts reported that agreement among his couples on various matters ranged between 76 and 89 percent.[7] In our sample, the extent of perceived agreement was not quite that high, but it was always at least 60 percent, and it was always higher among the happy than among the mixed and unhappy couples. Among the happy couples, the proportion of the spouses who perceived that they always or almost always agree was: 86 percent on making major decisions; 70 percent on handling family finances; 90 percent on career decisions; 68 percent on matters of recreation; 65 percent on dealing with parents or in-laws; and 61 percent on household tasks.

Again, it is important to note that a substantial minority on most of the issues indicated that they occasionally or frequently disagreed with their spouses. A satisfying marriage is more likely to have consensus across a broad range of issues, but a relationship can be satisfying even though there is disagreement on some issues. Consensus does not mean uniformity. Consensus does not mean loss of individuality. In a satisfying marriage, the consensus is sufficient to maintain the sense of being a couple, a solitary unit, but it is not so pervasive that it eradicates individual thinking. Furthermore, the consensus exists at the foundations, at the points that the spouses define as fundamentally important. As a husband said: "The things we agree on are much more important than the things we disagree on."

Happy couples tend to perceive agreement on things they consider of fundamental importance and tolerate disagreement on less important matters.

WE VERSUS ME

In both their communication and consensus patterns, the long-term, happily married couples deal with the dilemma of retaining individuality in an intimate relationship by keeping zones of privacy and by tolerating diversity. They discuss anything but they do not divulge everything. They agree on the fundamentals but do not insist on total consensus. They seem to recognize that it is important for each spouse to retain his or her separate identity. June, who works an an aide in a public school, has a satisfying, 25-year marriage. She advises:

Have interests you two share plus each should have individual interests. Don't become so lost in joint activities that you lose your individuality. Recognize that you are two separate individuals who hopefully have fun together and enjoy each other's company.

Similarly, Walt is a manager with a happy, 21-year marriage. He well expressed the ideal of retaining individuality while becoming a true couple:

We have blended two strong personalities into a family. By the choice of what we do and how we live, we try to emphasize the importance of our family and the values of life, which are important to us. I think we respect each other more. We try to accept more easily our uniqueness as individuals while yet blending.

Some of the respondents pointed out that they not only recognize the importance of individuality, but actually encourage independence and individuality in each other. They are aware that their relationship is enriched rather than threatened by the individuality of the spouse. As a teacher put it:

Being able to talk with each other and exchange ideas and share in the joy of each other's growth is what drew us together and has kept us deeply in love. I want all that is good for her to be hers. I value her differences from me. We are both deep feelers and very emotional, but she can be more logical and clear-headed than I can at times. We see each other as bringing different gifts to the marriage so that together we have much more.

In the parlance of the day, spouses in happy marriages tend to give each other "space."

Of course, the need for space differs from one person to another, so that there was variation among couples in terms of the extent to which they believed in individual activities. But there was considerable emphasis on the importance of accepting individual interests as non-threatening to the marriage: "We share interests but are comfortable doing things without each other at times if one doesn't care to participate"; "We each have some specific interests that we sometimes pursue which are understood by the other without it interfering with our marriage or our mutual interests"; "We have things we each do that the other doesn't, such as fishing. Our separate self interests add to our marriage, and the freedom to have these is important."

The separate interests may be something that one's spouse admires and appreciates, or something that one's spouse actively dislikes. One woman said that she and her 44-year husband were better friends than ever, but "I still have to leave the room when he listens to country music on television. I can't escape it in his car, but I won't have it in mine." On the other hand, Paula talked about the separate interests of her and her husband in much different terms:

We share interests in movies, legitimate theater, eating out, friends, and traveling. Each of us also has many interests of our own. But we both know something, and sometimes a lot,

about the interests of the other and each is understanding of the
interests of the other. These individual interests include such
things as photography, writing, bicycling, model airplanes,
painting, and our careers.

Some couples pointed out that they each have their separate
friends as well as mutual friends. One husband noted that he would
not have been able to handle such a situation when he was younger,
for his wife has male as well as female friends who are not his
friends. But he now finds it acceptable and, in fact, feels that it is
necessary for both he and his wife to have the freedom to maintain
some separate friendships.

The maintenance of separate interests, activities, and friends is
based on mutual trust, a sense of the importance of retaining one's
individuality, and the confidence that the individuality will enrich
rather than threaten the relationship. W. Robert Beavers has written
that healthy couples can tell "the difference between one person's
feelings and wishes and another's."[8] This capacity, he points out,
is crucially important if the marriage is to function well and be
gratifying to the partners. Therapists generally agree that healthy
relationships are those in which each person retains his or her
individuality. Our respondents also agree. They seem to be aware of
the necessity of not allowing the boundaries of their individual
selves to be lost in the togetherness of the marital relationship. They
trust each other sufficiently not to be threatened by their individual
pursuits. And, perhaps most importantly, they agree that each
should be free to have individual pursuits, indeed, should be
encouraged to have them. Faye is a receptionist who has been
married for 32 years. She finds value in some separate activities:

> We have increased appreciation of just being together, read-
> ing, riding in the car in silence, dining out, an evening of
> dancing, a day at an auction, and so on. But then we also enjoy
> our time as individuals. I think it's great when he goes to play
> cards or goes fishing with his male friends. I love the solitude.
> And I'm sure he enjoys his times of solitude.

Anne, a teacher's aide who speaks in near ecstatic terms about
her 17-year marriage, also realizes the importance and the benefits
of some separate activities:

My husband and I have mutual friends, but we also each have friends who are not really mutual. I'm glad my husband has several friends who enrich his life and help him to grow as a person. Then he has more to bring to me. And my husband feels the same way about me and my friends. We know that we each save the most special and wonderful parts of ourselves for each other.

Maintaining separate interests, activities, and friends can enrich the marital relationship if carried out in a context of mutual trust and agreement.

TOGETHERNESS VERSUS APARTNESS

On the one hand, it is not healthy for people to make marriage into a relationship in which there is a merging of identities. On the other hand, it is not healthy for the relationship if the two spouses maintain so much apartness that they are not truly a couple. Separateness can be as unhealthy as togetherness. Neither should be overdone. "I feel very strongly," advised a wife of 29 years, "that couples who go their own way and get so involved in activities that exclude the other person can easily grow apart. We have made an effort to do most things together." Similarly, a Missouri wife who has been married for 25 years said:

Over the years we have developed new and varied interests. Some have developed into hobbies which we can share and enjoy together. Instead of going separate ways, we seem to do more and more as a couple. I believe this has helped to strengthen our satisfaction with married life. In a successful marriage, it seems to me, the couple often think and act as one.

Note that she said "often" and not "always." Happy couples like to maximize the amount of time they spend together and the activities in which they share, but the do not strive for total togetherness or total sharing. The problem with most of the couples in our sample was too little rather than too much time together. Except for those in which both husband and wife were retired, there was a sense of never quite having as much time together as the couple would have preferred. In some cases, the time available was less than it had been previously. The demands of work or children's activities consumed an increasing amount of time. Those who faced that situation tended to report a diminished sense of happiness. They remembered with regret a period of their lives when they had more time to spend together. Thus, for many of our couples there was a desire for more togetherness. They had sufficient apartness, sufficient individual activities to maintain their separate identities. Many felt, on the contrary, that they did not have as much togetherness as they would have liked.

How much time is optimal? That will vary, depending upon the couple. As with so much else in marriage, the important thing is not an actual number of hours, but agreement between husband and wife. Our happy couples were much more likely than the mixed or unhappy couples to agree on the question of the amount of time they spend together (Table 6.2). What many agree on, however, is that they do not have as much time together as they would like. They prefer more togetherness. Such a preference is an indication of a satisfying relationship and of a desire for the marriage to last. Blumstein and Schwartz reported in their study of American couples that those "who spend less time together are less satisfied with their relationship and less committed to its future."[9] The marriage is less likely to survive when the two spouses pursue many individual activities.

What does togetherness mean? What is this thing that happily married couples want more of? In essence, it is more shared activities and more time as a couple. As in the case of apartness, the specific activities and the amount of time that are desired differ from one couple to another. The important thing is not that people do particular things apart and together, but that they do something apart and many things together. Togetherness can occur in many different facets of life. A California wife said:

> Marty and I are involved with each other on many different levels—love, family, work, recreation. Being good friends and all that that implies makes it all work well.

A husband of 15 years noted that he and his wife were "friends, lovers, income-earning partners, child-raisers, pursuers of recreation interests together" and various other things that all added up to a fulfilling relationship.

Togetherness tends to permeate the lives of long-term, happily

Table 6.2

Extent of Agreement on Amount of Time Spent Together

	Happy	Mixed	Unhappy
Always Agree	24.8	7.9	0
Almost Always Agree	50.5	36.5	13.2
Occasionally Disagree	21.0	36.5	42.1
Frequently Disagree	3.0	14.3	36.8
Almost Always Disagree	0.8	4.8	5.3
Always Disagree	0	0	2.6
	100.1	100.0	100.0

married couples. They work together on various projects, such as shopping, housework, and hobbies. One-fourth of the happily-married respondents said that they work together on a project at least daily, and another 63 percent said that they work on projects regularly together.

Just being together is meaningful. Activities or even conversations are not always necessary. We noted earlier that Faye, the receptionist, talked about riding together in their car as one gratifying form of sharing. Another woman said that she and her husband's quiet times together, their "quiet intimacy," was very meaningful to her. It didn't matter what they were doing, or whether they were doing anything. The "quiet, physical presence of my husband is relaxing and fulfilling," and that feeling had grown more intense over time.

The outcome of togetherness is a shared history of intimacy. The couple accumulates a store of shared experiences that are unique to them as a couple. Their unique history separates them from everyone else, even from their children. It provides each of them with the fulfillment of their intimacy needs (as discussed in chapter 2) and makes the relationship itself an increasingly rich and meaningful one. "The more things we share, the more memories we have together," said a Midwestern housewife, "and the richer the relationship."

Togetherness can lead to a shared history of intimacy that enriches both the individual spouses and their relationship.

DILEMMA OR OPPORTUNITY?

We began by posing the dilemma of union and individuality. How can spouses maintain their own identity and still become a true couple? How can they maintain both privacy and intimacy? As we have seen, happily-married couples fulfill both needs by having what we might call zones of freedom within a shared relationship. They communicate freely about any matter, but they retain the freedom *not* to communicate about some things. They agree on the fundamentally important matters, but they retain the freedom to disagree on some things. They try to maximize the time they have together and the activities that are shared, but they stop short at the boundaries of private pursuits. Togetherness is very important to them, but they recognize that it is two different people who are together. Indeed, those differences can enrich the relationship.

Thus, what appears to be a dilemma is actually converted into an opportunity for personal and relational growth. By affirming the importance of both the need for union and the need for individuality, our happily-married respondents report that they and their marriages are strengthened. Their lives as individuals and as couples are more meaningful because they accept the importance and necessity of fulfilling both needs.

ACTION GUIDELINES

If it is important to recognize that communication is not a cure-all for marital problems, it is also important to realize that a marriage cannot succeed without effective communication. We underscored the point that an individual cannot *not* communicate. There is an old story about a reticent New Englander who once confided to a friend that he loved his wife so much that it was all he could do to keep from telling her about it. There is more tragedy than comedy in the story. What the "strong, silent type" of people fail to realize is that when they do not talk about their feelings, others will attribute feelings to them. And they may attribute wrong feelings.

The erroneous attribution of feelings to one's spouse can lead to frustration and conflict. Consider the case of the man and woman who come home from work. She is cheerful and he is grim. He has had a difficult day at his work, but says nothing to her about it. She begins to think that she has done something or said something that has offended him. She finds herself getting irritated by his gloom and silence. She, after all, has also worked all day, and she would like to come home to a happy, supportive husband. She starts to snap at him. His response is finally to talk, but only to respond to her irritation with his own anger. Their entire evening may be ruined, and they may go to bed angry that night. They have added a distasteful experience to their shared history, though they may never know why. And it all began, not because of the lack of communication, but because of faulty communication.

It is important, therefore, for each spouse to recognize the fact that we are always communicating with each other and that a satisfying marriage depends upon managing our communication so that it effectively conveys what we wish it to. It is also important to recognize that an individual can learn to be an effective communicator. One way to do that is to learn the characteristics of effective communication. Barbara Montgomery, a communications expert, has suggested four aspects of what she called "quality communication" that are consistent with the patterns of effective communication practiced by our happy respondents.[10]

First, openness should characterize the communication. Openness is the willingness to engage in self-disclosure. As we have noted, too much as well as too little self-disclosure can be damaging to the marital relationship. Husbands and wives need to learn to talk about the things that are really bothering them. But they also need to use discretion. A spouse is not a therapist who can listen to

everything objectively. For example, it would not help the relationship for a man to confess to his wife that he feels lust for a female
friend of theirs. The total openness that is encouraged in the
therapist's office or in some small groups can be destructive to the
marital relationship. On the other hand, too little openness is also
destructive. Those who are married to a spouse who tends to be
reticent may have to help that spouse learn to be more open by
periodically encouraging and prodding the quiet spouse.

A second characteristic of effective communication is "confirmation," or an acceptance of the other. Confirmation in communication involves such things as eye contact, speaking directly to the
other, giving the other feedback that shows that one is listening, and
giving indications that one understands and accepts the feelings of
the other. Those who feel that there is too little confirmation in their
marital communication can engage in some exercises to correct the
situation.[11] One exercise is to require both spouses for two weeks to
acknowledge everything the other says and, in return, have the
acknowledgement acknowledged. This should be done no matter
how trivial the statement. If one spouse says, for instance, that it is
cold today, the other should acknowledge the observation some
way—"Yes, I noticed that it is cold also," or "You're right. I think
it's colder than yesterday." The first spouse would then acknowledge the acknowledgement: "So you noticed it too." This may
seem silly at times, but it is good practice in developing confirma-
tory communication.

Third, effective communication involves management of the
transaction. That is, there is an effort to control the course of the
communication rather than allowing the communication to control
the behavior and feelings of the individuals. For example, our
respondents noted that they try not to speak without considering the
impact of what they say. They know that certain things will hurt
their spouses. Therefore, as we shall discuss more fully in chapter
7, they advised against trying to resolve problems while one spouse
feels intensely angry. They know that people who are very angry
have difficulty controlling what they say, and the control of the
communication is very important if a satisfying relationship is to be
maintained.

Finally, "situational adaptability" is a characteristic of effective
communication. Adaptability means being sensitive to the appro-
priateness of the time and the place. It is not appropriate to unload
on a spouse in public. It is not appropriate to bring up an unresolved

problem when the spouse is very tired or hungry. It may not be appropriate to compliment a spouse in some public situations. A man who frequently talks about the beauty of his wife in public may be defined as an individual who is displaying his trophy rather than as one who admires his spouse.

A problem with establishing good communication in a marriage is the pressure of time. Particularly when there are children in the home, the varied demands may appear to leave little room for the couple to develop their own relationship. One couple solved the problem by insisting on having time each day, usually late in the evening, when they would sit and talk about the events of the day. Apart from an emergency, they did not allow their children to intrude upon their time together.

As this suggests, a couple has to work at being a couple. Like other facets of a satisfying marriage, good communication patterns do not necessarily come easily. People have to work at them. Our respondents repeatedly stressed the importance of marriage as work. Not only communication patterns, but consensus on important issues must be developed. They can be developed by working through differences in accord with the patterns of "good fighting" discussed in chapter 7. They can also be developed by setting aside time to discuss and establish rules in the home.[12] All couples have their differences. In our society, those differences tend to be intensified because of the changing roles of men and women. Americans do not enter marriage any more with a stable set of expectations about what it means to be a husband and a wife. Everything from sexual patterns to who takes out the garbage is subject to negotiation. A great many problems arise because of differing expectations about the rules and because each spouse assumes that the other should abide by his or her expectations. A more realistic expectation is that anything over which there is disagreement should be a matter of discussion and negotiation. Each couple must establish its own rules that are workable and acceptable to both husband and wife. Consensus between two people is neither the precursor nor the natural outcome of a marriage ceremony; it is the result of work.

The other characteristics of enduring marriages that we discussed in this chapter also involve work. A certain amount of time and energy needs to go into the maintenance of individual identities and activities. And togetherness must be cultivated—which means that it must be planned—in order to construct a shared history of intimacy. One way to cultivate togetherness is for each spouse to write down a list of things that he or she would enjoy doing during leisure times. The spouses can then share their lists with each other and each can check the things on the other's list that are appealing. Those activities should then be planned and pursued.

In some cases, each spouse may be reluctant to express a desire or preference for fear of being rejected by the other, or because of an unwillingness to make the decision and have the other less than fully pleased about it. As a result, they may spend as much time bantering about what to do in their leisure hours as they spend in shared activities. One couple said that they had problems deciding on which restaurant to go to when they ate out. Neither wanted to make the decision. They resolved the dilemma by agreeing to alternate in deciding where to go. Each also agreed to tell the other if a particular choice was undesirable for some reason. There are myriad problems in the effort to develop togetherness, but there are solutions to every one of them for the creative couple willing and determined to work at the relationship.

In sum, the business of becoming one flesh while maintaining one's individuality is a challenge to fulfillment that requires each spouse to engage in conscious effort. The Danish philosopher, Soren Kierkegaard, wrote an essay on love in which he noted that the marriage ceremony "is not a festive congratulation but a godly challenge, does not greet the lovers as victors, but invites them to a struggle."[13] Few, if any, couples achieve the satisfactions of a long-term marriage without fully engaging in the struggle. As one of the husbands in our sample put it, "A stable marriage doesn't just happen. It is designed."

FOOTNOTES

1. F. Philip Rice, *Contemporary Marriage* (Boston: Allyn & Bacon, 1983), p. 172.

2. Howard J. Markman, "Prediction of Marital Distress: A 5-Year Follow-Up," *Journal of Consulting and Clinical Psychology* 49 (No. 5, 1981):760–62.

3. Mark L. Knapp, *Interpersonal Communication and Human Relationships* (Boston: Allyn & Bacon, 1984), p. 251.

4. See Susan Singer Hendrick, "Self-Disclosure and Marital Satisfaction," *Journal of Personality and Social Psychology* 40 (no. 6, 1981):1150–59; and Arthur W. Pascoe, "Self-Disclosure and Marital Satisfaction," unpublished Ph.D. Dissertation, Case Western Reserve University, 1981.

5. William L. Roberts, "Significant Elements in the Relationship of Long-Married Couples," *International Journal of Aging and Human Development* 10 (no. 3, 1979–80):268.

6. Frank D. Cox, *Human Intimacy: Marriage, the Family and Its Meaning*, 3rd edition (St. Paul, Minn.: West Publishing Co., 1984), p. 151.

7. Roberts, *op. cit.*

8. W. Robert Beavers, *Successful Marriage: A Family Systems Approach to Couples Therapy* (New York: W. W. Norton, 1985), p. 78.

9. Philip Blumstein and Pepper Schwartz, *American Couples: Money, Work, Sex* (New York: William Morrow and Company, 1983), p. 183.

10. Barbara M. Montgomery, "The Form and Function of Quality Communication in Marriage," *Family Relations* 30 (January, 1981):21–30.

11. William J. Lederer and Dr. Don D. Jackson, *The Mirages of Marriage* (New York: W. W. Norton, 1968), pp. 277–84.

12. *Ibid.*, pp. 285ff.

13. Soren Kierkegaard, *Edifying Discourses* (New York: Harper Torchbooks, 1958), p. 183.

Chapter 7
Conflict:
How to Engage in ''Good Fighting''

Do those in long-term, satisfying marriages ever disagree? Do they ever get on each other's nerves? Do they ever consider divorce or separation? The answer to all three questions is yes. As Tables 7.1, 7.2 and 7.3 show, all couples have their times of turbulence and despair. Happy couples quarrel much less, are less likely to get on each other's nerves, and consider divorce or separation much less than those that are mixed or unhappy in their evaluations. But no one escapes problems. No marriage is totally free of conflict. Many people are unaware of the significance of conflict in a good marriage. In fact, they feel that disagreement means a poor relationship. In an experiment at a university, some undergraduate students watched actors portraying couples on videotape.[1] Some of the couples agreed on a topic under discussion and some disagreed. The students rated the couples who disagreed as having less affection for each other, being less compatible, and having a more unstable relationship. Conflict has a bad reputation. But enduring couples do not have conflict-free lives. On the contrary, conflict is an important dimension of their well-being. And that is because they have learned the secret of what someone has called ''good fighting.'' We will look at what ''good fighting'' means. But first, we need to see how conflict affects enduring marriages and why conflict is important to those marriages.

PATTERNS OF CONFLICT

What do people fight about? Obviously, we can have conflict over anything. But some issues are more likely to be a source of trouble than others. Sociologists Robert O. Blood, Jr. and Donald M. Wolfe surveyed over 700 couples in Detroit and found that the most common conflict was disagreement over money.[2] Their

Table 7.1

Frequency of Getting On Each Other's Nerves

(In Percentages)

	Happy	Mixed	Unhappy
All the time	0.2	0	0
Most of the time	0.6	1.6	13.2
More often than not	2.8	15.9	50.0
Occasionally	49.0	68.3	36.8
Rarely	43.7	9.5	0
Never	3.7	4.8	0
	100.0	100.1	100.0

sample of rural Michigan couples also revealed financial problems as the most common source of conflict. Following money, people were most likely to disagree about children, recreation, personality, in-laws, roles, religion and politics, and, finally, sex.

It was the first four areas—money, children, recreation, and personality—that affected most of the families in Blood and Wolfe's sample. These areas of conflict continue to be dominant ones. Financial conflict usually involves disagreement about allocation of the budget. Will we spend money for a new car or for something in the house? Will we purchase clothes for the children or pay off the doctor? Will we lend money to an in-law or use it for something for ourselves? The possibilities for financial disagreement are endless.

Conflict about the children is most frequent over the issue of discipline. How strict should we be? Should one or both parents be

Table 7.2

Frequency of Quarreling

(In Percentages)

	Happy	Mixed	Unhappy
All the time	0.4	0	0
Most of the time	0.4	3.1	7.9
More often than not	1.8	12.5	23.7
Occasionally	44.0	68.7	60.5
Rarely	51.9	14.1	7.9
Never	1.6	1.6	0
	100.1	100.0	100.0

Table 7.3

Frequency of Discussing Divorce, Separation
or Termination of the Relationship

(In Percentages)

	Happy	Mixed	Unhappy
All the time	0.6	1.6	5.4
Most of the time	0.2	0	5.4
More often than not	0.6	7.8	8.1
Occasionally	7.5	48.4	48.6
Rarely	43.6	28.1	29.7
Never	47.5	14.1	2.7
	100.0	100.0	99.9

responsible for meting out the discipline? Conflict over recreation involves the kind of activity each partner would prefer and the amount of time they spend together. Do we go bowling or to a movie? Do we spend all of our leisure time together or do we have a night out with friends of the same sex? Personality disagreements refer to various kinds of behavior of one of the partners that the other defines as immoral ("you should not drink so much"), irritating ("why are you so messy?"), or unacceptable or undesirable for some reason ("you don't think about my feelings"; "you worry too much").

Role problems, questions about who does what in the home and the marriage, did not affect a large number of the families in Blood and Wolfe's survey, but they affect an increasing number of Americans because of the changing role of women. In particular, the number of women entering the labor force, either to hold a job or pursue a career, has placed a strain on a growing number of families. There is a minimum of strain, of course, if husband and wife agree. But the typical pattern is for women who work to retain primary responsibility for taking care of the house and the children. Even men who encourage their wives to work do not always accept an equal responsibility for household matters. Many women are less than thrilled with such an arrangement, leading to conflict over rights and responsibilities.

The things that people fight about are not the same at all stages of their relationship nor is the frequency of fighting likely to remain constant. The couples in Blood and Wolfe's sample reported somewhat differing kinds and amounts of disagreement, depending upon how long they had been married. Those in the honeymoon phase had more disagreements about personality differences and about how they would spend their recreational time. For those beyond the honeymoon period, conflict over money was the most common problem, though there were fewer disagreements over money among those in the empty nest and retired phases than those in earlier stages of their marriages. And there was less conflict of any kind among couples in the later phases of their marriages.

What we have said thus far applies to those in long-term, happy marriages as well. That is, the couples in our sample did not have enduring marriages because they escaped the kind of serious problems that others face. On the contrary, they have had some of the same problems, the same conflicts, as everyone else. Jane described her fifteen-year marriage as "perfect" now. But she also talked of the way in which her parents had a "devastating" impact on her marriage in the early days, of her husband getting involved with another woman, of the end of her dream of a "Prince Charming and Cinderella" relationship, and of the therapy that finally renewed the dying marriage. Others told us about the same range of problems—from infidelity to excessive drinking on the part of one of the mates to arguments over everything from money to in-laws—that are typical of American couples. A number of our respondents noted that there were times when they were near divorce. Some have chronic problems that are a permanent part of the marriage:

> My wife's health was bad for many years, creating many problems in raising the children. At times, she could not cope with them, and it was difficult making choices between her and the children as well as between her and my family whom she never liked and refused to see. Life was hard for her when the children were young. It took all her time. I often felt torn between my wife's needs and the children's. I still have to try to keep peace between my wife and our children. She has difficulty relating to her son-in-laws.

People who have been happily married for a long time, then, are not necessarily more problem-free than others. They experience some of the same difficulties and disagreements as everyone else. But they also know the importance of confronting the problems head-on. They know that there is no utopia to which they can flee. As a woman married thirty-one years said in response to our question of what advice she would give to others:

> Problems do arise and must be faced. The most important thing is to face them, work them out. Do not run home to Mama! Consider your marriage as a lifetime commitment. Do not at any time feel that it would be easier to just get a divorce. The problems you have are your own and will not be solved by quitting. Hang in there. It's worth it.

The confronting of problems is seen in the response to the question of how often one of the spouses leaves the house after a fight. That is an avoidance tactic that people in happy marriages seldom use (92.1 percent, compared to 56.3 percent in mixed and 36.8 percent in unhappy unions said they rarely or never leave). Thus, a first principle of conflict is:

> *Those in long-term, happy marriages have the same kind of conflicts as others, but they view them as challenges to overcome rather than as signs of deterioration or failure.*

THE IMPORTANCE OF GOOD FIGHTING

One woman had no problem acknowledging that she and her husband had conflict. "Of course we do," she said. "Our marriage is worth fighting for." She recognized one of the important reasons for fighting—to save a valued match. We noted in chapter 3 that some marriages are "devitalized." They may continue formally, but they have no life. The couple is not really involved with each other. Their relationship is on a dead-end course. Their marriage is, as one marriage counselor put it, simply dying of dry rot.

In other words, one of the benefits of conflict is that it prevents the dry rot that slowly corrodes a relationship. Conflict is a refusal to let the relationship deteriorate. Two marriage counselors who have written about the value of conflict point out that the great majority of the couples who come to them do *not* engage in conflict.[3] In fact, the couples avoid fighting. The result is not peace, but an emotional divorce. Ironically, the refusal to fight disrupts rather than cements the union.

Not all fighting is "good" fighting, however. Conflict *can* kill a marriage. We will detail below the elements of "good" fighting identified by our respondents, the kind of conflict that enhances rather than destroys a marriage. In essence, good fighting has rules and aims at a win-win outcome. The rules establish limits to what is acceptable in a conflict. Good fighting is never of the "no-holds-barred" type. And good fighting also aims at a win-win outcome, which simply means that both partners win as a result of the conflict. Most people tend to think of conflict as a win-lose situation. One person beats the other, so that someone is a winner and someone is a loser. But conflict can be of three kinds: win-win, win-lose, and lose-lose. People who have happy long-term marriages have learned how to engage in win-win conflict.

We should note here that there is no standard prescription for engaging in conflict. There is no single way to fight that is useful for all couples. For one thing, all of us have personal styles of conflict with which we feel comfortable. Social scientists have identified at least five different personal styles.[4] These styles differ in terms of how concerned we are for ourselves and for the people with whom we have conflict. One style is competition, which is a high concern for self and a low concern for others. The person who has this style views conflict as a kind of war, where the point is to win rather than to be concerned about the opponent.

A second style is avoidance. Avoiders have little concern for either themselves or for others. They do not pursue their own interests—at least their interests in the relationship at hand—nor do they concern themselves with the interests of others. As we noted above, avoidance is one way to kill a marriage.

Third, there is compromise. Those who compromise are concerned about both themselves and others. Their self-concern is tempered by their concern for others. Thus, they are willing to find a solution that is satisfactory rather than optimal. They assert themselves, but they always moderate their demands in order to arrive at some point of mutual satisfaction.

Collaboration is a fourth style. Collaborators are the opposite of avoiders. They have a high degree of concern for both themselves and for others. They pursue their own interests avidly while maintaining a high degree of concern for the interests of others. The result is that they tend to negotiate in order to find creative solutions to problems. The collaborator does not merely want to compromise, to find a middle ground that is acceptable to both. Rather, the collaborator wants both parties to the conflict to be fulfilled.

Finally, accommodation, the fifth style, is the opposite of competition. The accommodaters neglect their own interests in order to allow others to be fulfilled. Accommodaters will engage in conflict, but they will always go along with the wishes of the other or others.

Each of us tends to adopt one or the other of the above as our personal style of conflict. We do not necessarily follow a single style rigidly, however. For instance, an individual who is generally accommodating might take a collaborative or even competitive stance on a particular issue that he or she regards as of fundamental importance. Obviously, not all of these styles are conducive to a good marriage. Some combination of collaboration, compromise, and accommodation would seem to be the most likely style to use for good fighting. The style used by those in enduring marriages, as we shall discuss below, is mostly a combination of compromise and accommodation. Whatever the styles of the people, however, they always follow the principles of abiding by rules and aiming at a win-win outcome.

Conflict can save a marriage from dry rot.

Good fighting means following mutually acceptable rules in conflict in order to obtain a win-win outcome.

THE NATURE OF GOOD FIGHTING

Even though we cannot provide a standard prescription for good fighting, there are certain principles that were mentioned time and again by our couples. These principles provide the guidelines for fighting that insure a win-win outcome.

Maintain Your Perspective

Maintaining a perspective on conflict simply means to keep in mind that not everything is worth fighting about. "We don't treat every incident as a disaster," said one man. Steve, a corporate manager married for three decades, talked about his own perspective:

I'm not by nature a fighter. But I will fight if I feel the issue is worth it. I guess that there haven't been many issues that I feel are worth it in my marriage. We've had very few fights. We both would rather make love than war. So if a disagreement comes up over, say, something like whether we should buy some new furniture, I tell her to go ahead even though I don't feel we need it. Why should we fight over a few dollars for furniture? Sometimes I give in and sometimes she gives in. We just feel that most disagreements aren't as important as our good relationship.

Of course, sometimes when people fight over relatively trivial issues, the conflict is symptomatic of some deeper issue. But there are also some individuals whose basic style is competitive, as we described it above. They have a tendency to make every issue a win-lose situation and to fight in order to insure their own victory. The happy couples in our sample, by contrast, distinguish between those issues that are trivial and those that must be resolved through conflict. They don't try to make a battle out of every skirmish. They save their fighting energy for issues that are really important.

Trivial issues should be distinguished from important ones; many things are not worth fighting about.

Develop Tension Outlets

Sometimes conflict is a result of issues between partners and sometimes it is the result of external frustrations. Stuart Chase once wrote about a New Yorker who stalked out of his house one morning and greeted the first man he met with a punch on the nose. The victim happened to be a detective, who arrested the man and took him to the police station. The man's explanation for his behavior was simple: he had had a disagreement with his wife and he felt like hitting somebody.[5] Chase pointed out that the incident underscores the point that a good deal of conflict between people has its roots in something outside their relationship.

Indeed, problems with your spouse can make you angry and hostile in your dealings with outsiders. But it is also true that problems with outsiders or with situations can make you angry and hostile in your relationship with your spouse. More than one man or woman who is frustrated at work comes home and takes it out on a spouse or children. And there are sufficient frustrations in the world in which we live that we all need some outlets for the tensions that build up.

Couples who have a long-term, happy relationship seem to sense the need for tension outlets in order not to make each other the victims of their frustration. One woman told us that we all need regular physical exercise in order to deal with our tensions and prevent them from affecting our marital relationships. A husband suggested that all couples get away by themselves on a regular basis, even if it is only for a few hours. And a wife noted that a sense of humor not only "helps one keep a balance" but also "helps to relieve tension." A number of people mentioned the value of maintaining a sense of humor even during conflict. The humor, they noted, can put the conflict into perspective and neutralize any damaging effects.

Each person must discover what is his or her own best tension outlet. One person's tension outlet is another's tension trap. Some people play golf to relax, for example, while others get frustrated and angry. You have to discover for yourself what works for you. But it is important to make that discovery. Otherwise, you may find yourself having conflict with your spouse when the real problem is the frustration and tension you have built up from something or someone outside your marital relationship.

Tension outlets are important to minimize conflict due to external frustrations.

Avoid Festering Resentment

The noted psychiatrist, Karl Menninger, related the odd story of Harry Havens, a man who went to bed and stayed there for seven years with his eyes covered because he was angry with his wife.[6] According to the news report of the incident, Harry liked to help his wife with household tasks. When she reprimanded him for the way he was doing one of them, he became angry. He told her that he was going to bed for the rest of his life. ''And I don't want to see you or anyone else again.'' After seven years, however, he decided to get up because the bed became uncomfortable for him.

If there is such a thing as a perfect pout, Harry would probably get the award for it. Few people carry out their resentment to such extremes. But many people have the problem of letting an argument slip into a cold war of festering resentment. By contrast, those in enduring marriages know the importance of openly confronting issues and resolving them. They do not allow their conflict to continue indefinitely on a cold or hot basis.

Open confrontation means an honest sharing of feelings between partners. You don't make your spouse guess what's on your mind or what you are feeling. We are all very prone to misinterpret each other's feelings and behavior. Roy Pneuman and Margaret Bruehl point out that one of the first steps in effective management of conflict is to distinguish between our awareness of situation and the way in which we interpret the situation.[7] That is, we see certain behavior or certain appearances, and we interpret what they mean. But our interpretations may be quite distorted. As an example, they tell of an incident in the early days of the civil rights movement. Some black and white leaders in a small southern community decided to get together to see if they could resolve some of their differences. A woman who was regarded as one of the primary leaders among the black delegation got up at a particularly tense point in the discussion and walked out. One of the white men, fearing that something had been said to offend her, ran after her. She assured him that nothing was wrong. She had just been chewing her tobacco too long and had to spit it out. In any effort to manage conflict, it is important not just to observe the behavior of others, but to put a correct interpretation on it. Obviously, the only way the white man could have known the meaning of the black woman's departure was to ask her. All speculation about the meaning would probably have been counterproductive at best.

The same problems occur in marital relations. A wife notices that her husband appears grim. She assumes that he is angry with her for some reason. A husband notices that his wife is withdrawn. He assumes that she feels no affection for him for some reason. We continually interpret each other's behavior in order to know how to respond. But our interpretations may be quite wrong. The husband may be frustrated by his work. The wife may be preoccupied with her work. If they don't ask each other, if they don't tell each other, they will continue to make wrong assumptions. And wrong assumptions can lead to resentment. The way to avoid that is simple—an honest, open relationship. As one husband of 27 years put it:

> We have learned to work out disagreements, which is necessary for any two people who live together for any length of time. I don't believe that there are any built-up resentments between us, because we've always been honest. We haven't tried to make each other guess.

A number of our couples talked about one particular method they use to openly confront problems, to avoid festering resentment. They follow a pattern of not going to bed while they're still mad. A man married 26 years said:

> Early on, we decided never to go to bed with unresolved conflicts. We lost a lot of sleep! Seriously, we *talk* out instead of *walk* out. I would urge young people to review their philosophy of marriage and if it is one that believes in stability and commitment, they should look beyond the immediate crisis to the long view. Is the small crack or hole in the dam worth plugging or will it be allowed to expand until the dam breaks? Even *tiny* problems must be worked out together.

Another husband, an educator married for 29 years, told of one of his early experiences.

> Shortly after we were married, we had a fight about something and I went to bed angry and frustrated. I don't remember what the argument was about. But I remember very well laying there in the dark and seething on the inside. Suddenly, Betty

began to whistle. I said, "What in the world are you doing?"
She told me that she didn't think we should go to sleep while
we were angry. So we turned on the lights and worked it out.
It's a great rule to follow.

On an even more positive note, a husband of 34 years said that not
only should you not go to bed angry, but you should close each day
with an expression of affection: "Regardless of what garbage
you've been through, take and hold each other close and give thanks
that here's someone who wants me."

*Festering resentment can be avoided by openly confronting
differences and an honest sharing of feelings.*

Be Sensitive to Timing

The comedian, the lover, the psychiatrist, and the political leader
all know the importance of timing. The same event, the same
statement, the same behavior can all have very different consequences depending upon the timing. Our respondents pointed out
that timing is also important in marital relations.

Timing with regard to conflict simply means that there are certain
times when it is best to avoid conflict and other times that are
appropriate to confront it. Openly confronting conflict does not
necessarily mean immediate attention to an issue. Some people are
more receptive to problem-solving in the morning and some in the
evening. Few if any people can handle conflict well when they are
exhausted. In addition, there are times when it is simply inappro-
priate to raise an issue. The wife who criticizes her husband's
appearance just as they are walking into a party, or the husband who
angrily tells his wife in front of friends that she neglects his needs
both illustrate insensitivity to timing.

A number of our happily-married respondents added a point that
is not as obvious as the above. They said that people should not try
to solve their problems while they are very angry. "Take time to
cool down," said a woman who is very happy with her 21-year
marriage. She indicated that it isn't necessary to solve things while
you are angry, that, in fact, you probably can't solve anything at
that time. We will return to this point in discussing the kind of
communication that is important in good fighting.

The outcome of conflict depends in part upon appropriate timing.

Communicate Without Ceasing

All of the things we said about communication became of paramount importance during conflict. Of course, it is almost trite to say that communication is an imperative to effective conflict management. But two things need to be said about communication that are not trite. First, it is not a cure-all. Communication can reveal unlikeable as well as likeable qualities about others. Furthermore, communication may reveal unresolvable differences of opinion on some issue. Thus, while communication is important in managing conflict, it will not eliminate conflict and it will not create universal love. Our respondents stressed the importance of communication—"talk, talk, talk," said one with emphasis—but they did not see it as a cure-all apart from the other principles we are discussing in this chapter.

Second, the *kind* of communication is as important as the bare fact of communication. Simply talking to each other is not necessarily communication. Those in enduring marriages emphasized two qualities of communication that are important in conflict management. One quality is reciprocity. Communication must involve both an active giving and an active listening. The other quality is calmness.

Reciprocity in communication during conflict means active listening as well as open expression of your own ideas and feelings. We emphasized above the importance of openly expressing your own feelings to your mate. But the listening is likely to be even more of a problem than the expressing. To actively listen to someone else during conflict requires you to give the other person full opportunity to express himself or herself and also to strive to understand exactly what the other is saying. We tend to put most of our energies during conflict into making sure the other person hears and understands us. It is equally important to make sure that we hear and understand the other as well. One of our respondents said that she uses the technique of repeating what her husband says during an argument to check if she really understands his point.

Active listening demands not only that you understand the other, but also that you understand what the other thinks you are saying. As one wife said: "You must understand what your mate is saying and what he thinks you are saying.'' In other words, you listen in order to determine whether you are effectively communicating your own ideas and feelings.

People who learn to listen as well as to express themselves will find that conflict can be a creative force in their marriages. Sandra is a sales representative who has been married for 27 years. Her experience of conflict has basically been a positive one:

> I have two cartoons on my refrigerator. One says, ''Happiness is knowing you are married to your best friend.'' The other says, ''Love is listening before criticizing.'' Listening to each other. Trying not to lose your temper. We have found that when we have opposing viewpoints, we discuss each other's ideas and let the subject rest awhile. We think it over. Many times we have found that each of us had persuaded the other to our point of view. So now we have two good ideas. We just have to figure out which one is the best. It's now not my idea versus your idea. It's *our* idea.

Effective communication during conflict involves not only active listening but also a certain calmness. There is one school of thought today that emphasizes the expression of our aggressive feelings. One therapist recommends that, while dating, women should not hesitate to be a ''real bitch.'' They need to get rid of their hostilities, he says. They should tell their dates where they're at. ''Let it be total vicious, exaggerated hyperbole.''[8] Others have suggested that married couples similarly let out all the stops in their conflict (short of physical violence). Partners, they say, should freely vent their anger with each other. Others, however, point out that while expressing hostility in a therapist's office may be helpful to an individual, it does not necessarily follow that scenes of rage will benefit a family. It is one thing to tell a therapist that you hate your spouse at times, and another thing to tell it directly to your spouse. Moreover, the research of a number of social scientists indicates that the expression of hostility and violence in a family tends to bring about additional aggression rather than peace.[9] And the higher the level of verbal aggression, the more likely there is to be physical aggression as well.

Which of these positions is correct? Is aggression a catharsis that gets rid of your hostility and restores harmony in the marital relationship? Or will aggression simply increase the likelihood of future aggression? We pointed out above that our couples stressed the importance of open, honest communication. However, that does not mean that each partner is totally transparent to the other. They do not advocate that you "let it all hang out" in conflict. Quite the contrary. They come down squarely on the side of those who emphasize the damaging effects of aggression in the home. Mel is a salesman with two children and a 36-year marriage. He feels strongly about the proper way to handle conflict:

> Discuss your problems in a *normal voice*. The first person that raises their voice—stop. Return after a short period of time. Start again. After a period of time both parties will be able to deal with their problems and not say things that they will be sorry for later. I believe if I lose my temper I will lose the argument.

Similarly, a woman who has 33 years of marital experience advises nothing less than a calm discussion:

> Talk to one another, but not when you're angry. If you have an argument about anything, stop and think before you open your mouth. Find something to do until you are both calm, and then talk things out.

Only one of our happily married couples advocated anything other than a calm discussion. One husband said that he and his wife yell at each other when they fight. "We yell out our frustrations at each other," he said. "Once we get them off our chest, they no longer bother us and we forget them." Everyone else disagreed. This simply underscores the point that there can be no universal prescription for handling conflict among couples. But the bulk of happily married couples agree that calmness is the only way to fight and have a win-win outcome.

Effective communication during conflict requires active listening as well as expressing, and calmness rather than aggression.

Be Flexible and Willing to Compromise

Sociologist Georg Simmel, who made an extensive study of human conflict, called compromise "one of mankind's greatest inventions.''[10] Our happily married couples clearly believe in the importance of accommodation and compromise as styles of conflict. They seem to combine the two, giving in at times when they do not regard the issue as important and willingly compromising when the issue is one that matters more to them. They do not view compromise as surrender, but rather as the only realistic way to handle differences. For they repeatedly told us that one of the important ingredients in a long-term relationship is tolerance and respect for differences. If you have tolerance and respect for your spouse, your aim is to find a solution that is acceptable to both of you rather than to determine which of you is right. There may be some issues that have a right and wrong answer (clearly, for instance, there are some right and wrong ways to discipline children), but most issues are judgment calls. Thus, the point of conflict is not to be victorious over your mate, nor is it usually to determine who is right in the matter. The point is to find a resolution that is satisfactory to both of you. As one woman told us, "Don't expect to solve all problems. Cope with them. Be flexible in your approach to problems."

Compromise implies an equal amount of "give" by both parties. But those in enduring marriages know that you must sometimes be sufficiently flexible to go more than 50-50. There are times when one of the partners may be under particular stress, or have special needs for some reason. The appropriate course then may be for one mate to give more than he or she receives. This is the second-mile compromise, a willingness to do more than is expected, to forego the 50-50 ideal in order to meet the needs of the other. Some of our respondents even talked about the second-mile compromise as an attitude of mind that should characterize each partner. A woman happily married for 44 years told us that she would advise all young marrieds to "be willing to give 70% and expect 30%." A husband married 31 years said he was extremely happy in his union. He noted that many people talk about each partner giving 50-50 in a good marriage. But, he said, "I believe if each gives 60-60 and expects only 40 in return, it can't miss." By contrast, a woman who was a little unhappy in her 23-year marriage said: "Our marriage is a 60-40 proposition. I give in, because he is the breadwinner."

Flexibility, the willingness to compromise, and the willingness to go the second mile are essential elements of good fighting.

Use Conflict to Attack Problems, Not Your Spouse

Many people feel such a distaste for conflict that they think of it only as a destructive force. Indeed, conflict can be quite destructive. Verbal aggression can shred people's confidence, destroy their hope, and rob them of any ability to trust others. But not all conflict is destructive. People can engage in conflict without hurting each other. They can use conflict to resolve problems rather than to harm each other. Attacking problems rather than your mate is fundamental to good fighting.

Our respondents suggested two things to do to keep the conflict focused on problems. One is to define the conflict as a disagreement over some issue rather than as a personal attack. Sherri has been married for 26 years. She is a part-time music teacher who regards her union as extremely happy. She told us that it is very important "to look at conflicts as mere differences of opinion and not as threats to one's personal integrity." Even if your mate attacks something you do or say, you must recognize the difference between an attack on some habit and an attack on you as a person. Steve, the educator, pointed out that it took him some time to realize this difference:

> When she would correct my eating habits, I thought she was despising me as a person. When she glared at me for something I said to someone, I thought she was showing her disgust for me as a person. One day I realized that she only did those things because she loved *me*, even though she didn't like some of the things I did.

When you distinguish between an attack on a problem and an attack on yourself, you can more easily do the second thing that happily-married people suggest: resist the temptation to hurt your mate. Our respondents were particularly emphatic about the need to avoid letting conflict degenerate into an "insult session," as one called it. They are sensitive to the need to avoid saying things or doing things that they will later regret. No matter how angry you are, no matter how intense the conflict, warned one husband of 27 years, you must "always add to her self-esteem. Never tear her down." When conflict degenerates from an attack on an issue to an attack on persons, it leaves scars that are difficult to heal. The conflict tends to become self-perpetuating, a contest of one-upmanship in verbal insults. Keeping the focus on the problem rather than on each other will result in the partners feeling good about themselves and each other. The conflict will enhance rather than corrode their closeness.

There is a close link between this principle and the principle of calmness. Happily-married people seem to recognize that it is much easier to blurt out insults or lash out angrily at your mate while you are angry. One husband, therefore, advises others to ''say cool'':

> Bite your tongue and never say anything to your spouse that might linger or persist. If you want to inflict hurt, you can with words. Angry words persist. When both spouses are cool, reason seems to prevail.

> *Good fighting involves an attack on problems, not on people; good fighting resolves problems and builds up people at the same time.*

Keep Loving While You Are Fighting

Loving and fighting may sound like contradictory activities. To many people, fighting means that there is an enemy, or at least an opponent. And we don't normally think about loving enemies or opponents. Nevertheless, it is possible to both fight and to love. You must keep in mind the meaning of love as we defined it in chapter 5, for love includes a concern for the well-being of the other independently of our feelings at the moment.

Our respondents agree that you can love and fight at the same time. In fact, they agree that it is important to do both. Conflict is no reason to stop loving. How do you continue to love someone while fighting with them? We have already discussed one way—refusing to hurt the other during conflict. A husband of 25 years suggested a second way: ''Try to keep on liking the other person and try to help each other without rewards.'' This is the flip side of avoiding hurtful words. Put forth effort to positively like the mate with whom you are fighting and to help him or her. And how can you do that? Sherri, the part-time music instructor, has a method:

> It is important to continue to let your mate know that you still love him even though you differ with him in some area. When we are involved in some kind of a difference, I try to focus on

all my husband's good points, rather than his negative ones. I find this immensely helps in resolving differences.

Her method may or may not work for others. The point is that it is possible to love (always keeping in mind that love does not depend upon current feelings) even while fighting. Love helps turn conflict into good fighting, so that both partners win.

In good fighting, love—an active concern for the well-being of the other—continues to characterize the relationship.

ACTION GUIDELINES

It helps immensely to know what is typical. As a father of three children said:

> We found that the child development books we read greatly eased the concerns we had about our own children. It was a great relief, for example, to know that children typically are out of bounds around the ages of two-and-a-half and four years. Our children had not gone berserk after all! They were simply typical.

One of the ways to deal with conflict constructively is to recognize that it is typical. Those in long-term, happy marriages have the same conflicts as everyone else. When conflict occurs, therefore, it should not be regarded as a sign that the marriage is deteriorating, or that the couple has made a mistake, or that the marriage is in jeopardy. On the contrary, people need to view conflict like those in enduring marriages—as a challenge that can actually enhance and solidify the relationship if the couple engages in good fighting.

Those who want to engage in good fighting may have to change their perspective and/or their typical style of conflict. Those who think of conflict as a win-lose process need to accept the fact that both partners can win and to determine to make all conflicts win-win situations. Those whose style has been competitive or one of avoidance can profit by the advice of our respondents and try to develop a compromising and accommodative style. A collaborative style should also work very well. Our couples did not generally use collaboration, perhaps because it requires considerably more energy and time than the others. It may not be worth the trouble in most cases.

Accommodation is best when the individual considers the issue trivial. We need not fight about everything. We can accept some things that we would not necessarily prefer. As one of our female respondents, extremely happy in her 15-year marriage, said:

> Talk about things that *really* bother you. Try to accept each other's eccentricities. If you think he does strange things, think of some of the things you do.

People must keep in mind, however, that it is important to be sensitive to the feelings of one's mate. One of the spouses may consider something trivial that the other regards as quite important. We can accommodate ourselves to our mate's wishes in the matter without indicating to him or her that you feel the whole thing is trivial.

It is always helpful, and it may be very important, for people to analyze their arguments. If a couple is having too many arguments and/or they have not been win-win fights, it will be useful to recall as many of them as possible and analyze them in terms of the principles of this chapter. For example, has either of the spouses viewed conflict as inherently undesirable or as a sign of a problematic marriage? Has each distinguished between trivial and serious issues? Are the conflicts rooted in external tensions? Have the spouses developed tension outlets? Has the timing of the confrontation been appropriate? Is either spouse troubled by resentment because he or she hasn't honestly shared his or her feelings?

Resentment is a festering sore to a marriage. It can be avoided by openly confronting differences and sharing feelings. But some people have great difficulty in sharing their feelings. Some require professional help. It is also possible for people to help each other. For instance, a man or woman whose spouse has difficulty with this can try saying such things as: "You seem angry today. Is anything bothering you?" "It is important to me to know how you feel about this matter. I can't deal with it when I'm puzzled about your feelings." Of course, such tactics will not obtain instant results. Some people grew up in families that discouraged or even punished the expression of feelings. Some people may need professional help before they are able to let others know how they feel. But sometimes a husband or wife can help a spouse to overcome a reluctance to express and share feelings by continuing to stress the importance of the behavior.

Nothing is more important, and perhaps nothing is more difficult, than listening as well as expressing oneself during conflict. In fact, active listening is a skill that many people have never learned. We once heard a sales manager complain that too many salesmen have "two mouths and one ear." Most of us are familiar with the individual who looks at you while you are speaking but obviously never hears what you are saying.

If listening is so important, and if it is a skill, how can it be learned? We have to work at it. We have to decide in advance that we will actively try to understand what the other person is saying. This may require us to hear the other out rather than interrupting and responding too soon. We may have to repeat what the other has said to verify that we have understood him or her. That is, an individual should feed back what he or she thinks the speaker has said and let the speaker confirm its accuracy. We need to watch for feelings as well as for words. Are the feelings appropriate to the words? If not, the real message is deeper than the words would indicate. We need to observe the nonverbal behavior of the other. What does the smile, the shrug, the pitch of the voice, the posture of the body indicate? Of course, it is best to practice the skill of listening in all of our interaction rather than to apply it only when we are in conflict.

We underscored the importance of a calm rather than an aggressive discussion. Jane, extremely happy in her 35-year marriage, suggests a technique for married people to use in conflict:

> They need to learn to talk over conflicts in a non-aggressive way. They should express their ideas and feelings without attacking the other person. Say: "When we arrived late at the dinner party last night, I felt embarrassed and uncomfortable," rather than saying with anger, "You always make us late everywhere."

In other words, it is a mistake to begin conflict by laying the blame on the spouse. Rather, people should tell each other how they feel as a result of each other's behavior. That is a non-aggressive way to engage in conflict. It is a way of attacking the problem rather than the person.

Some couples may be helped by role-reversal techniques. That is, in engaging in a particular conflict situation each agrees to try to

take the role of the other for a period of time. Role reversal is a good
way to see if each really understands the position of the other. For
example, a couple having a dispute about the budget can say in
effect: "Okay, let's see if we really understand each other. I'll argue
this from your perspective and you argue it from mine." Each has
the opportunity to correct any deviations from his or her perspective
in the spouse, and also is likely to get a better sense of the spouse's
perspective. Role reversal can help people reach an acceptable
compromise in the face of an apparent stalemate.

According to virtually all of our respondents, calmness is vital for
constructive conflict. What can an individual do who remains calm
but whose mate remains very angry? There is a piece of advice in
the Book of Proverbs that is supported by modern social scientific
knowledge: "A soft answer turns away wrath, but a harsh word stirs
up anger." An angry response to anger is like trying to quell a fire
by throwing gasoline onto it. Calmness as a response to anger,
however, will usually quiet the anger of the other.

Finally, the way to make conflict into a win-win situation is to
continue to keep the well-being of the other in mind. That means
swallowing those words that will hurt the other before we let them
out. It may mean a willingness to go the second mile, to give more
than we receive in a particular instance. Those who strive for a happy
and long-term relationship will make it their aim, in all conflict, not
only to resolve the problem but also to build up their mates.

FOOTNOTES

1. Norman Epstein, Debra Finnegan, and Diane Bythell, "Irrational Beliefs and
Perceptions of Marital Conflict," *Journal of Consulting and Clinical Psychology* 47
(1979):608–610.
2. Robert O. Blood, Jr. and Donald M. Wolfe, *Husbands and Wives: The Dynamics of
Married Living* (Westport, Ct.: Greenwood Press, 1978), pp. 240–41.
3. G. R. Bach and P. Wyden, "The Art of Family Fighting." Pp. 314–20 in K. W.
Kammeyer, ed., *Confronting the Issues* (Boston: Allyn and Bacon, 1975).
4. Joyce Hocker Wilmot and William W. Wilmot, *Interpersonal Conflict* (Dubuque,
Iowa: William C. Brown, 1978), pp. 27–32.
5. Stuart Chase, *Roads to Agreement* (New York: Harper & Bros., 1951), p. 18.
6. Karl Menninger, *The Human Mind* (New York: Alfred A. Knopf), p. 213.
7. Roy W. Pneuman and Margaret E. Bruehl, *Managing Conflict: A Complete
Process-Centered Handbook* (Englewood Cliffs, N.J.: Prentice-Hall, 1982), pp. 11–13.
8. Quoted in F. Philip Rice, *Contemporary Marriage* (Boston: Allyn & Bacon, 1983),
p. 215.
9. *Ibid.*
10. Georg Simmel, *Conflict and The Web of Group-Affiliations* (New York: Free Press,
1955), p. 115.

Chapter 8
From Nowhere to Somewhere:
Avoiding the Ruts

A young man, puzzled by his wife's desire for a divorce after only three years of marriage, said that as he reflected on his marriage he realized something important. While nothing critical seemed to have happened, the relationship had been "going nowhere" for some time. He and his wife had gotten into a rut, a rut of weary sameness in their relationship. As we have noted earlier, some marriages do not fall apart because of dramatic spasms of fighting, but because of the subtle corrosion of indifference or neglect. There may be no intense or even specific problems that plague the relationship. The marriage is simply going nowhere, and the people involved in it are one day struck with the fact that they are weary of nowhere. As we pointed out in our discussion of the passive-congenial and devitalized marriages in chapter 3, some couples *remain* in the rut of nowhere. But those who create a fulfilling as well as an enduring union have learned how to keep growing. Their marriage is going somewhere. It is a vital, developing process.

How do people avoid the ruts? The question is important because there are many marriages that last but do not fulfill. In their survey of American marriages, Blood and Wolfe wrote of the "corrosion of time" that wears away the "strengths in marriage."[1] In their sample, 52 percent of wives were very satisfied with their marriages in the first two years. After twenty years, only 6 percent were still satisfied. How do some people avoid slipping into the rut of dissatisfaction? Among our happily married couples, there are three aspects to a long-term relationship that seem to be particularly important in maintaining vitality. For one, the relationship must involve two changing people, who are changing in a direction that enhances rather than disrupts compatibility. Second, there must be a process of mutual education throughout the relationship, in which each teaches and helps change the other. And third, there are certain "small" things that enliven the relationship, particularly humor, playfulness, and spontaneity. We shall look at each of these elements in some detail.

YOU'RE NOT THE PERSON I MARRIED

Every marriage is a relationship that involves two changing people. Virtually everyone can say of a spouse, "You're not the person I married." Among those in long-term, happy marriages, however, that statement is a cause for celebration, not lament. If variety is the spice of life, then being married to a changing individual is an adventure that enhances the quality of life—*if* the person is changing in a desirable way, of course. One man spoke of his 17 year marriage as a shared adventure in growth. "We are more deeply in love; our friendship grows as we affirm each other's growth . . . We grow more satisfied each day. Growth is what our marriage and our lives feed on." A wife of 15 years ventured the thought that "almost one-hundred percent of the changes in us and our marriage have been positive and have increased our satisfaction with our marriage." A Georgia man was similarly positive when he pointed out that he and his wife had changed many times but that "each new level brings an increased satisfaction in our marriage."

It isn't that all changes are good or desirable or edifying for a relationship. But change is inevitable, and two people can change in a direction that makes them more rather than less compatible, more rather than less enamored of each other. Moreover, the changes can help maintain real vitality in the marriage. For in a real sense, it is like being married to a series of different people without losing the continuity and stability of a long-term relationship. One man said that he felt that he had had five different wives in 33 years. Another said that he and his wife had each been "creatively married" to somewhat different people as each of them changed through the years.

People, and therefore relationships, inevitably change over time, but the change can be in the direction of enhanced compatibility and vitality.

The Creativity of Time

As the above indicates, among our long-term, happily-married couples, time was a creative rather than a corrosive factor. In contrast to the unhappily married, the great majority of the happy spouses indicated that their mates were more interesting to them than when they were first married (Table 8.1). One woman responded to the question of why her 32-year marriage had lasted by saying:

I would give only one answer. It is the culmination of all. My husband is more interesting to me now than when we were first married—in *every* facet of our relationship as man and wife, as friends, and so on. Yet he still has a mystery about him, a privateness that intrigues me.

The reason that a spouse becomes more exciting and intriguing over time, of course, is because he or she changes into a more inter-

Table 8.1

Percent of Responses to: "My Mate is More Interesting
Than When We Were First Married"

	Happy	Mixed	Unhappy
Strongly Agree	53.8	18.8	5.3
Agree	32.0	23.4	15.8
Neutral	10.3	37.5	23.7
Disagree	3.4	17.2	36.8
Strongly Disagree	0.6	3.1	18.4
	100.1	100.0	100.0

esting person. Jack has been married for 20 years. He says that he gets a great deal of satisfaction from the achievements of his wife. But she was not always involved in activities that enhanced her appeal, nor was she always easy to talk to about various matters: "She's more interesting to me now than in earlier years because her defenses are significantly less in a lot of areas like child-rearing, career, and running the household. We now have a more positive dialogue."

Time is a creative factor in a second sense—the relationship can get more comfortable. It is important to keep in mind that comfort is only one aspect of the creativity of time. For comfort alone can be boring. But comfort combined with change can be exciting. Of her 32-year marital relationship, Evelyn noted that the most important change was a "gradual being more comfortable and sure of the reactions of the other person." The awkwardness of the dating situation and the adjustments of the early years of marriage can give way to a sense of security and ease. Again and again our respondents underscored the importance of getting to know the habits and quirks, the strong and the weak points, the likes and the dislikes, the flexibility and limits of each other. It is this interpersonal understanding that can only come through interacting over a period of time that gives the relationship its comfortable aspect.

Finally, then, time is creative in the sense that the relationship of long-term, happily-married people becomes more mature. Over time, our couples learned to be more tolerant of each other, more open with each other, and more accepting. Paula, a housewife who is "extremely happy" in her 18-year marriage, said that her marriage had become more open in the sense that there were fewer games being played between her and her husband. "We are learning to be ourselves, and accepting ourselves and each other." Another wife summed up the creativity of time by pointing out that the 29 years of her marriage involved a process of attaining a more comfortable, mature, and fulfilling relationship:

> We have become much more tolerant of each other's quirks of personality. We know who we are. Often we can predict the other's reactions to events or attitudes. The relationship has sweetened over the years. I wouldn't change places with anyone I know.

Time is a creative rather than a corrosive factor when a spouse gets more interesting because of his or her changes, when the

> *relationship gets more comfortable because of increased
> understanding, and when the relationship matures into open-
> ness and acceptance.*

Personality

Psychologists have debated about whether personality alters in any fundamental way over time. Most accept the doctrine of stability, but during the 1970s a number of challenges to the traditional view appeared. In a review of the evidence, Zick Rubin noted that there is undoubtedly a "tension between stability and change" in each of us.[2] We each strive to maintain our identity over time, but we also strive to become something more or different than we are. Continuity and change are equally important to us. That dual striving can account for the fact that longitudinal studies show strong relationships between earlier and later characteristics but not an unchanging personality structure.

In any case, our respondents perceive certain changes in personality which they felt enhanced their relationship. Some of them said that no *major* changes had occurred. But there were changes, and they were important to the relationship. One of the more common changes mentioned was a "mellowing" over time, which means to them a smoothing out of some of the rough edges of personality.

One aspect of mellowing is increased tolerance and acceptance. In contrast to the stereotype of the aging person as one who becomes more inflexible, more "fixed" in his or her ways, our respondents saw each other and themselves as becoming more tolerant, more accepting over time. In particular, this mellowing applies to their relationship. That is, our respondents see both themselves and their spouses as more willing to accept each other's flaws. One woman said: "We haven't changed as much as I might like," but she had become more accepting of her husband: "his 'warts' are less important than they were years ago." Jack, a Midwestern husband of 33 years, said that both he and his wife had become "more tolerant and accepted the idea that everyone has some quirks and faults." A wife stressed the fact that the tolerance extends to some habits "that we know will never change, so we don't try to change them."

Still, mellowing does not mean that one simply learns to live with undesired qualities. Our respondents not only saw themselves and their mates as more tolerant and accepting, but also as more tolerable and acceptable. In other words, mellowing means to them that they can tolerate flaws more but also that they have less serious flaws to tolerate. "I have better control of my temper than I did in the early years," said one husband. "She has become more understanding and patient. Our relationship is more strongly based on trust and confidence." A wife pointed out that her husband's mellowing meant that he was "more considerate of me as an individual."

We might be inclined to ask whether the mellowing refers primarily to increased tolerance or fewer rough edges in the personality. Our couples suggest that both things have happened. Each undoubtedly reinforces the other.

In addition to mellowing, our respondents pointed out some other ways in which they and their mates' personalities had changed. The changes were not dramatic, but they were in a direction that made the relationship more satisfactory. A college professor said: "I have become less self-centered, less goal-oriented, less obsessed with anything. She has become more confident and more relaxed." A number of others saw themselves or their mates as becoming less self-centered, more considerate of others. In each case, the change made the marriage more satisfactory, for in each case the person- ality change was defined as evidence of increased concern for the relationship. That is, our respondents define each other as moving from a self-focused to a relationship-focused personality. They avoided, or at least had moved out of, what we might call the Rakitin syndrome. In Dostoyevsky's novel *The Brothers Karam- azov*, Rakitin was a man who "was very sensitive about every- thing that concerned himself" but he was "very stupid about the feelings and sensations of others—partly from his youth and inexperience, partly from his intense egoism."[3] Those who are afflicted by this syndrome can find neither self-satisfaction nor marital happiness. As a more recent observer has put it:

> By concentrating day and night on your feelings, potentials, needs, wants and desires, and by learning to assert them more freely, you do not become a freer, more spontaneous, more creative self; you become a narrower, more self-centered, more isolated one. You do not grow, you shrink.[4]

In the eyes of our respondents, they and their mates have grown because they have moved in the direction of increased concern for others and for the well-being of their relationships.

Personality changes enhance marital satisfaction when they are defined as a mellowing or as moving toward an increased concern with others, particularly with the marital relationship and the spouse.

Roles

Role changes are an inevitable part of human existence. Some of the role changes among our respondents were typical of many long-term marital relationships—becoming parents, assuming a work role, adjusting to the empty nest. Our respondents defined many of these developmental role changes as enhancing their relationship. For example, they typically viewed the "empty nest" as a positive factor in the marriage, allowing the couple to recapture some of the freedom and fun of the early days of the marriage.

Interestingly, there were also role changes of the type that sociologist Ralph Turner called "role-making," a process of change in a particular role over time.[5] The wives in our sample were not untouched by the woman's movement and the changes in woman's roles that occurred during the 1960s and after. In fact, one of the more common role changes was that the women had become more independent and equal and assertive over the course of the marriage. We noted in an earlier chapter that those in long-term marriages must work through the problem of retaining individuality while becoming "one flesh." Among our respondents, one way to work through the problem was for the woman to reject the traditional role of submissive housewife. Margaret, a wife of 15 years who went back to school, illustrates the process:

> My attitude toward marriage changed from being a housewife and having my wishes subverted. Now my wishes as a person are important. I'm no longer the typical housewife. We share responsibilities. He's more tolerant and understanding of me broadening my horizons. We value our time together more and make sure it's quality time, leading to increased stability and happiness.

Margaret was married at a time when the woman's movement was strong. But even women married at an earlier time, when traditional expectations prevailed, have changed. Amy is a school

teacher who was married at the dawn of U.S. involvement in World
War II:

> When we were married in 1941, I was the sheltered, dependent
> wife typical of that era. Over the years, particularly because I
> was the sole parent during the war years, I have become a
> self-sufficient, much more assertive person. After being a
> homemaker for twenty years, I returned to my career of
> teaching and have derived much satisfaction from it and
> believe it has invigorated our marriage. Sometimes, though, I
> feel my husband is jealous of my outside activities and friends.

Amy notes a potential fly in the ointment of marital bliss—the
husband's reaction to the changed role. So far, that has not
adversely affected her marriage. Some couples find that the husband's feelings about the new role of his wife may create some
difficulties, but the problem is not insurmountable. One man said he
was "very happy" in his 33-year marriage in spite of the fact that
he and his wife disagreed about her career choice: "All of our
children have left and she is now in real estate. That has resulted in
some conflict, but it's really my problem and not hers."

Generally, the men have accepted the changed roles of their
wives. They support the change through their behavior. A woman
who reported herself as "extremely happy" in her 32-year marriage
noted that both she and her husband had changed in their roles. She
related the way in which she became more independent by going
back to work after her son grew up:

> I assert myself more now, especially when it comes to
> spending money. He now helps more with the household
> chores so we can spend leisure together, which he didn't do
> when our son was young. He left all household duties to me
> and he went out without me. He's kind of changed with the
> times.

Ralph, now retired, says that he was a "typical male supremacist"
and his wife of 35 years was "a meek little housewife" when they
married:

> We both felt I should earn the money and she should stay
> home. I am now a firm believer in ERA, share the house work

with her, and so on. My wife has a part-time job and does some volunteer work. I encourage her to do both. Our marriage is better today than ever.

The woman's movement has been blamed at times for contributing to the high rates of divorce in recent times. Our respondents point out, however, that the aims of the movement can be realized without marital disruption as long as both spouses accept the change. In fact, the kind of independence and equality attained by women like those discussed above is probably a vital part of marital satisfaction. There is strong evidence that the restrictive nature of the traditional role of the married woman in American society creates stress and leads to the high rates of physical illness and emotional disturbances among those women.[6] Women who expand into new roles after their children are grown are less likely to have problems of depression in their middle years. And those who have supportive and understanding husbands are unlikely to encounter marital difficulties as a result of their changing role.

We should note that the important thing is not that every woman should become more independent and assertive by pursuing a career, but that every woman should be free to choose. Some of our respondents remained happy as housewives. One woman, for instance, said that the difficult time of her life was when her children were growing up and her husband was working long hours. Now, however, she is happy with more free time and more money to spend: "With six kids and no car, I was trapped for many years. But I fulfilled my obligations and now am enjoying the rewards." She has no desire for a job or career, only for freedom of movement. Others, however, found it necessary to pursue some kind of work or career. A wife of 20 years said that she and her husband had become "a lot closer, a lot more intimate" as a result of her working part-time and becoming less dependent upon him. The important thing for a woman's well-being is freedom of choice. The important thing for marital satisfaction is a supportive husband.

Role changes contribute to marital satisfaction when both spouses define them as desirable.

The freedom to make role changes is essential to marital satisfaction.

Aims and Goals

A number of couples pointed out that they had changed in terms of what life goals they considered important. In particular, a number had become less concerned with material success and more concerned with interpersonal success. The important thing here, as in so many other areas, is that the couple define their changes as compatible with each other. That is, as long as both change in the same direction the change makes the marital relationship more solid. As we shall see in the next chapter, one of the elements identified by couples as important in their successful relationship is agreement on aims and goals in life. The crucial thing for a happy relationship is not having a particular set of aims and goals, but having agreement on whatever aims and goals are chosen.

The importance of agreement is underscored by one of the wives whose 15-year marriage, though still rated by her as happy, has reached some troubled times:

> My husband has done a complete career change. He sold our business and now is a truck driver. This makes me feel embarrassed in front of friends. The children are also embarrassed by it. I went back to school and have less time for him. Our marriage has been good until now. He is tired and wants to semi-retire and live on our boat. I don't want to give up my financial goodies and I am just ready to get started in a career of my own. It's like we are at opposite spots. It feels like he wants to kick back and die and I want to live and get out there and accomplish things.

Of course, it is unlikely that each spouse's aims and goals will change at the same time and in the same direction. When they diverge, however, the couple can work at bringing them back into line. As a wife who is "very happy" in her 21-year marriage said:

> Our goals have changed as far as work is concerned. This requires that we be good listeners for one another and be resilient enough to weather growth and change. I feel our relationship has become more satisfying as we grow through good and bad times together.

Thus, if aims and goals diverge for a time, a couple must work to achieve compatibility. Otherwise, the prospects for long-term satisfaction are dim.

For long-term marital satisfaction, spouses need to work at making their changes in life aims and goals compatible with each other.

Interpersonal Skills

Partly as a result of "good fighting" (chapter 7), those in long-term, happy marriages see their interpersonal skills as improving over time. They feel that they have improved communication with each other and that they are better at dealing with situations of conflict. "We talk more when things bother us about each other," said one wife. "We don't let our tempers get the best of us. The changes have increased the satisfaction of our marriage."

None of our respondents claimed to have superior interpersonal skills at the time of marriage. Such skills developed over time. Our respondents stressed the fact that a good marriage is a matter of patient work, not something that one gets in a package deal by choosing the right mate. Andy, a retired white-collar worker, said he was "very happy" in his 40-year marriage, but he was not always adept at handling conflict:

My wife and I have always had a good physical relationship and we've always been able to talk—eventually. We had to learn how to argue productively. That took the first ten years. I used to clam up and that would drive Dottie nuts. I wouldn't talk to her. I finally learned that that was punitive. We had professional counseling at one point about ten years into our marriage. We almost broke up, but didn't.

Marital satisfaction increases when spouses work at improving their interpersonal skills.

Affection

Even where their sexual activity has diminished, the respondents report a deepening of their affection for each other over time. "We like to spend more time with just each other," said one wife. "And at home. Sex is not as important; companionship is now more important." A Georgia man, "extremely happy" in his marriage said: "We have become better friends, where for many years we were more of lovers."

A deepening of affection, like the other changes we have discussed in this section, underscore the point that "you're not the person I married" can be a cause for celebration rather than lament. In some cases, the changes have not been as extensive as one of the spouses would have preferred, but any amount of change is helpful. One couple, each of whom was very happy with the 33-year marriage, agreed that one of their problems had been the man's difficulty in expressing his affection. "I don't show it enough," he admitted, "but that's the way I am. She should know that I love her without me constantly showing it. I do a better job now, though; we almost never disagree on this anymore." His wife had a similar perspective on the situation:

> He demonstrates affection more now than he used to. I once said to him, 'You don't love me anymore.' His reply was: 'I told you once that I love you, and when I don't anymore, I'll let you know.' He is doing more now, and I understand more how he feels.

Affection can deepen over time even if sexual activity decreases.

Changing Together

One of the important marital tasks is the management of change. Change is inevitable. As the philosopher, Alfred North Whitehead, put it, "no static maintenance of perfection is possible . . . Advance or Decadence are the only choices offered to mankind. The pure conservative is fighting against the essence of the universe."[7] The impetus to change comes from both within the individual and without. The changing world in which we live will have a differential impact upon each spouse, because each spouse is to some extent in a different as well as a similar segment of that world. A marriage, then, is composed of two changing people who are engaged in a changing relationship in a changing world. The way in which a couple manages those changes is crucial.

As we have indicated, the most important thing about changes is that they are in a direction that makes the couple more rather than less compatible. This can only be done if both spouses accept the necessity for change both in themselves and their mates. One of our unhappy wives underscored this in describing the source of dissatisfaction in her 17-year marriage:

I don't need to be as dependent as I did when I was younger. I need more independence and more experiences outside of the house. I'm not as content with being a housewife. But my husband hasn't changed. He still wants me to continue in a traditional role and not spend time outside the house.

Another wife pinpointed one of the major problems in her "twenty-one very hard years of marriage" as the fact that at the time of her marriage her husband told her "that any changes that would have to be made would have to be made by me and not him." In contrast, our happy couples noted the way in which they supported and enjoyed the changes that were going on in themselves and their mates.

The road to marital fulfillment would be easier if all couples had the experience of one who said their aims and goals had changed over time, but "no matter how they've changed, we always seemed to have been going in the same direction." For most couples, the direction will not always be the same. The point then is to work at bringing the diverging directions back into line. In particular, it is important to manage change in a way that the spouses ultimately are going in the same direction. As one California wife put it:

What has made my marriage work for me is being able to change and grow together. Not as a separate unit, but as a pair. It has always been very much a part of my life to have communication going and never let it go. Talk to each other, discuss family and business matters. Being married for over 27 years hasn't been easy. We certainly have had our ups and downs. But each one of these is a lesson and you learn from it and make it work for you. I can honestly say that now I am about the happiest I have ever been in my married life. My children are grown and my husband and I are really enjoying each other.

*One of the important marital tasks is the management of
change; satisfaction will depend upon managing change in a
way that maintains or enhances compatibility of the spouses.*

THE POWER OF MUTUAL EDUCATION

Since the kind of changes outlined above helped vitalize the
marriages of our respondents, the question arises: what factors were
at work in their lives to bring about such changes? Undoubtedly, as
we noted, there were many. But one of the most important is the
spouse himself or herself. In long-term, happy marriages, there is a
process of mutual education. The conventional wisdom, that you
don't marry someone with the intent of reforming him or her, is only
partially true. Among our respondents, each partner teaches and
helps change the other. As Mel Krantzler wrote in his book,
Creative Marriage, one of the challenges of marriage is "to become
a friendly teacher and receptive student to each other."[8]

Indeed, a certain amount of "re-forming" of one's mate is not
only possible but essential if the direction of change of the two is to
be towards greater compatibility. Those who neglect the challenge
of mutual education, of helping each other to change in mutually
desirable ways, may imperil their relationship. Consider Jim and
Marilyn, a young couple with whom we counseled. After their
infant daughter died, they had a difficult time adjusting. They began
to have marital problems. The relationship was very strained when
they talked with us. At one point Marilyn admitted that much of
their trouble was related to their problems in accepting their
daughter's death. "There are times," she said, "when I just want
Jim to take me and hold me close for awhile." Jim looked at her
with some surprise. "Did you ever tell him that?" we asked.
"No," she admitted. "I wanted him to realize that I needed it and
do it without asking." As it turned out, Jim was more than willing
to fulfill her needs, but he needed to be educated to be sensitive to
them. And Marilyn needed to be educated to be more open to Jim
about her needs. Their failure to teach each other intensified their
problems.

Our happily-married couples underscore the power of mutual
education to enrich a relationship. But just how much can people do
with each other? Our respondents do not claim that one person can
totally reform another. There are some problems that may be

beyond the capacity of a mate to change. A wife who was unhappy with her 45-year marriage commented on the fact that she had been able to do little other than survive her husband's alcoholism:

Problems with alcohol can't be solved. You never know if you did the right thing by sticking it out. My children have always wanted me to get a divorce. They blame me for their problems with their father.

Obviously, there are limits to what one can do with a spouse. But our respondents indicated that there are also some rather significant changes that can be effected through the process of mutual education in a marriage. Over time, an individual learns how much can be done. "Everyone changes over time . . . You learn how far to push each other and know when to back off," said a man who had 28 years of a happy marriage. In general, the "push" that our respondents gave each other was gentle but made a significant difference.

The marital task of mutual education is essential for directing the process of change in a direction of greater compatibility.

Changing Attitudes

Some of the changes were attitudinal. Gerry, married for 18 years, worked as a sales representative when he and Denise said their vows. He was 22 and she was 19. Their initial problems stemmed from the fact that she was devoutly religious and he had some serious doubts about spiritual matters. They were married by a judge. Gerry described in detail how Denise discovered very soon that she had married a "chauvinist" and how she gradually changed him. At first, she accepted his tendency to be "king of the castle" because she had been brought up by a stern, though fair and caring, father. She did not think of herself as one who should be making any decisions about the home or the marriage. Gerry had reenlisted in the service because of financial problems. They were stationed in Hawaii when he first realized that she was less than happy with their marriage:

What should have been an idyllic three-year tour in Hawaii was misery for Denise and frustration for me. I pursued those interests that I had always wanted to become involved in—golf, sailing, and scuba diving. She stayed home caring for our first child and having a second. I often wondered why she seemed so unhappy. Didn't she have two beautiful children to take care of and a husband who got one promotion after another? The background for "revolution" was set during my assignment to an isolated place in Alaska. This meant that I had to leave Denise and the boys at home in New York. Her initial anxiety about having to make the decisions on a daily basis was soon overcome by the sense of pride she developed in her new-found abilities. By the time the year was over and we were settled in our new home in England, Denise was ready to tackle the chauvinistic idiocy of "no wife of mine will ever work." She did it gradually at first, by just helping out at the landlord's store across the street. Then we moved to California. She proceeded cautiously by working part-time as a Red Cross volunteer in the hospital. I accepted this because my role as the breadwinner was not threatened because she was not earning any money.

My next assignment was in New Mexico. I had become dimly aware that Denise was happier when she was allowed to have an identity outside the home. Denise began to work part time. Then she worked full time. I didn't oppose it. She convinced me that I would be much happier with a human being for a mate than a robot. We now have more open communication and we negotiate important issues. Denise continues to be tactful and diplomatic as she helps me overcome the remaining vestiges of chauvinism, and I continue to encourage her to further her own education and development.

Gerry's account illustrates an important point made above—in his eyes, Denise's pushes were very gentle. She was obviously concerned about his feelings. But she demonstrated to him that their relationship would be far better as his chauvinism diminished and her development proceeded apace. She has educated him to the point where he defines his prior attitude as undesirable and harmful. Her method was one of demonstrating to him in gradual steps that a different attitude would benefit them both, as individuals and as a couple.

Mutual education results not only in the diminishing or shedding of attitudes defined by a spouse as undesirable, but also in the development of attitudes defined as preferable. A husband of 27 years said that his wife had come from a large family where she had learned how to compromise. He did not have that trait when they were married, he noted, but *"I have learned."* He underscored each work. His wife had helped him develop what she regarded as a most important attitude about the way to handle differences.

An important point to keep in mind with all of the changes that result from mutual education is that the couple is essentially engaged in the process of making each other more attractive, more likeable individuals. Taken out of the context of respect for the other and the maintenance of individuality, mutual education could sound like mutual manipulation. But in context, the process of mutual education means that each spouse is married to someone who increasingly is the kind of person that that spouse prefers to be with.

Changing Personality

There were a number of ways in which our respondents perceived their personalities, or the personalities of their mates, as changing through the process of mutual education. Among other things, they mentioned greater self-awareness, more assertiveness, reduced hostility, and increased sensitivity. Elizabeth is a librarian who has been married for 30 years. She believes that her husband helped her to change in a fundamental way:

> My spouse has always been a confronter and I was brought up to believe it was wrong to express negative feelings. My spouse has given me acceptance of my real self with its warts and blemishes and I have learned to assert myself in a straightforward manner . . . My husband and I have a tough love in that we enable each other to be our best selves. I feel that we are both growing stronger, and even though there are some growing pains connected with it, my satisfaction with our marriage has increased.

Similarly, Bill, a successful manager, noted how his wife of more than 25 years had helped him to change:

> When I was younger, I was very insecure, unsure of myself. One day when I was bemoaning my fears of failure and inadequacy, she told me that she really admired men who were

strong and self-confident, and that she herself needed to have a husband like that. She said it in a way that made it sound like a request, not a put-down. She told me that she thought I was very competent and very strong, but that I needed to act more that way. I determined from that day on that no matter how I felt in a situation, I would try to appear strong and self-confident. I did, and I have become that kind of person.

Husbands and wives can use mutual education to help each other develop the kinds of attitudes and personalities that enhance their attractiveness to each other.

Educating for Maturity

How does the process of mutual education occur? We have noted that there is a "gentleness" associated with it. The mutual education described by our respondents was usually more of a gentle prod, a reminder, an encouragement, than a challenge or rebuke. And it includes a modeling of the desired attitudes or behavior, teaching in deeds and not merely in words. As one husband pointed out: "I've become more sensitive to the needs of others for two reasons. She not only reminds me quietly when I am insensitive. But she is one of the most sensitive, caring people I have ever met. Her example inspires me."

The result of this mutual education may be not only changed attitudes, behavior, and personalities, but also a maturing of the individual. A number of our respondents attribute their personal growth as individuals to the influence of their spouses. They also see their spouses as more mature because of what they have done. "We are two neurotic people who stumbled into each other's arms and grew up emotionally together," said a California woman who was "very happy" with her 23-year marriage.

As people become more mature, of course, their attractiveness increases. Again, the outcome of the process of mutual education is a higher degree of marital satisfaction. As a social worker put it:

> We married when we were eighteen, against the wishes of both families. He was very immature. But we grew up together in our marriage. After we had one child, we put each other through graduate school. We are devoted to each other, and I can't imagine coming home from work and him not being there.

Mutual education in marriage is a process of gentle instruction and modeling.

When mutual education leads to perceived growth in maturity, marital satisfaction is enhanced.

THE ROLE OF HUMOR AND PLAY

As Table 8.2 shows, happily-married couples laugh together far more frequently than those who are unhappy. Nearly three-fourths of our happily-married respondents said that they laugh together once a day or more. And as we shall show in the next chapter, shared humor is rather high up on the list of reasons why happily-married couples believe that their relationship has endured. We were frankly surprised by the extent to which our respondents emphasized the importance of humor. Yet, on reflection it becomes obvious that humor can keep variety and enjoyment in a relationship. People who laugh together are obviously not suffering from the rut of boredom.

Humor should be understood in the broad sense here as including playfulness. The importance of playfulness is underscored by the research of R. William Betcher, a clinical psychologist.[9] In his studies, Betcher found that playfulness has an important function of stabilizing a marriage. It helps couples avoid the extremes of alienation and overwhelming intimacy. In other words, it is a way of achieving the ideal we discussed earlier, of maintaining individuality while still becoming one flesh. In addition, playfulness can enhance communication, strengthen the marital bond (we tend to value most highly the playful relationships we have), and minimize the possibility of destructive conflict (humor can be a safer approach to a sensitive topic). When play disappears, Betcher observed, it may be a signal that the marital relationship is disintegrating, and the resumption of play may indicate that a troubled relationship is healing.

Our respondents concur with Betcher's analysis. They rank humor as an important element of their enduring relationship. ''One thing that allowed our marriage to endure,'' noted one wife, ''is my husband's outstanding sense of humor, his ability to make me laugh.'' ''Laughter is a steady diet here,'' said a husband of 26 years as he explained why his marriage succeeded. ''Our kids are funny and so is most of life. One needs a satiric eye in order to survive.''

Table 8.2

Frequency of Laughing Together

(In Percentages)

	Happy	Mixed	Unhappy
More than daily	34.7	7.8	5.3
Once a day	38.1	25.0	28.9
Once or Twice a Week	23.7	37.5	23.7
Once or Twice a Month	1.8	25.0	26.3
Less than Once a Month	0.8	4.7	13.2
Never	1.0	0	2.6
	100.1	100.0	100.0

Humor and play are ways of demonstrating happiness. An astute wife pointed out that "this communication of happiness is very important to the relationship." To engage in humor and play with one's spouse is to say, "I enjoy being with you and sharing fun times together. You make me happy and I want to make you happy." Grace has been married for 25 years. She emphasized the importance of sharing in her marriage, including humor:

Humor and seeing humor in everyday things is necessary to the enjoyment of life. And laughter is even more enjoyable when shared with someone else who sees the same things as humorous. Shared laughter is an important kind of sharing.

Humor and play are important in troubled times as well. As one man said of his 22-year marriage, "Humor really helps. The ability to laugh and play, to be like kids almost, helps through the hard times." And a Missouri wife who said that her marriage was "wonderful" agreed that humor had been a great help in coping with troubled times: "Laughter relieves tension and a sense of humor helps one keep a sense of proportion. Laughing together, as well as struggling together, helps to strengthen bonds. But without laughter, the suffering seems pointless."

Humor and playfulness strengthen the marital bond and help couples to cope with difficulties.

ACTION GUIDELINES

Falling into a rut of boredom with the relationship is one of the more insidious threats to marital satisfaction. It is ironic that some couples can avoid the wrangling conflicts that afflict many disintegrating marriages only to find that the dry-rot of boredom has eroded their bonds. To the question of whether boredom can be averted in the long run, the answer of our couples is a resounding yes. We all change, and we can change in a way that makes our relationships more vibrant and more compatible. The challenge that people face is to manage change so that the outcome is a stronger and more satisfying relationship. Three important tools that our respondents identified in that task of managing change is a proper attitude toward change, mutual education to guide the course of change, and the maintenance of humor and play to keep the process lively and enjoyable.

First, it is important to have an appropriate attitude about change. A professional man related an incident from his family life that occurred when his daughter was about five years old. He went into her bedroom to tell her good night and found tears on her cheeks. "What's the matter?" he asked her. "Nothing," she said. "I was just thinking how happy we all are, and I hate to see it change." The father explained to her that there would be much happiness ahead for all of them, and that if they didn't change they wouldn't be able to stay happy. The father was trying to teach his daughter that, as Whitehead noted, the static maintenance of perfection is not possible. We will change. We must change. Once we accept the inevitability of change, we can effectively manage it by developing the appropriate attitudes. Research suggests that the attitudes needed are to view change as normal, as desirable, and as a challenge rather than a threat. People can develop such attitudes as they come to realize that change *is* normal, desirable, and a challenge. One way to develop such attitudes toward change is to use the self-instruction techniques that we discussed in chapter 4. That is, we can continually remind ourselves that change adds zest to life, and that the outcome of change can be a new level of maturity and fulfillment. This is not a process of self-delusion; as we have tried to emphasize, development, growth, and advancement are all processes of change, and few if anyone would want to stop such processes. As the couples in our research clearly say, a relationship can change over time towards greater meaning and fulfillment. Those who attempt to keep things just as they are will rob themselves of the potential for a more interesting, more comfortable, and more fulfilling relationship.

There are two kinds of change that the couple will confront. One is the change that is in some sense imposed. It may be an inevitable change, such as aging or retirement. It may be a change that is happening in society, such as the changing role of women. It may be an organizational change, such as a new boss that makes the job of one of the spouses stressful. The other kind of change is that which one or both of the spouses initiate (the mutual education process). In either case, the change must be managed, which is to say that the people must play an active role in dealing with the change rather than passively acquiescing to it.

Mutual education is an important way of managing the direction of change. While maintaining respect for the integrity of each other, couples can help change each other's attitudes, goals, behavior, and even some aspects of personality. By each spouse being both teacher and student, the relationship becomes stronger because the spouses become more compatible. The important thing, as we noted above, is to be ''gentle'' in the educational process. Gentleness implies a concern for the other rather than a desire to control the other. Some people try to change others by using threats. There are, to be sure, some situations where a threat is needed. An individual who has an alcoholic spouse, for example, may need to frankly state the consequences (marital breakup) if the offending spouse does not get professional help. Others use ridicule, which can backfire. For example, a wife who keeps telling her husband that he is boorish (ironically, in the hope that by telling him he will somehow change) may convince him; he may accept that definition of himself and continue to act in a boorish fashion. A husband who attempts to help his wife develop more skills by continually telling her that she is mechanically inept may find that she accepts his definition and keeps on being helpless in the face of any mechanical task. Many people do the same with their children. They say, "You are so clumsy," or "You act so dumb," or some such statement that is supposed to alert the child to a deficiency and make him or her resolve to correct that deficiency. The outcome, for a spouse or a child, frequently is not a correction but an acceptance and continuation of the behavior. After all, if someone that important in our lives and that knowledgeable about us tells us that we are a certain kind of person, is it not true?

The point is that effective mutual education must focus on the positive. Rather than saying, "You are so boorish," the wife might say, "You can be the kind and thoughtful person that I admire so much, but sometimes you tend to forget. You were very rude the other day." Rather than saying, "You are so dumb with anything mechanical," a husband might say, "You are so intelligent about other things, I know that you can manage some of these mechanical tasks." Sometimes the education can be indirect by pointing out the qualities that one admires in those of the opposite sex generally. This must be done in an appropriate fashion so that the spouse does not take it as a put-down or a negative comparison with someone. For example, one wife noted that she made a point to her husband as they were discussing a movie they had seen. She thought the leading man was extremely attractive and he thought the leading man was less physically attractive than others he had seen. "Ah," she told him, "but it isn't just physical attractiveness that is important. He was strong but kind and sensitive. That's what I find attractive in a man." She made her point. And she made it without resorting to a humiliating comparison like "Why can't you be kinder and more sensitive like Jim?"

One thing that is very important in the process of mutual education is recognition and reward of the desired behavior. When the husband, for example, actually behaves in a kind and thoughtful way, the wife should note that and tell him how much she appreciates it.

In addition to the instruction, of course, each spouse can model the appropriate kind of behavior. Mutual education that is positive, gentle, and modeled will lead to increased compatibility and enhanced satisfaction.

Finally, humor and playfulness are very important to maintain vitality and joy in the changing relationship. Humor and play can be an important part of the process of mutual education when the subject is a sensitive one. But they are also important in their own right. For some people, humor and play seem to come easily and frequently. Others might have to cultivate them or consciously work at bringing them into the relationship. A wife of 29 years, "extremely happy" in her marriage, said: "I look for humor to share with him—from life, from books and magazines, from everywhere." Those who can't create their own humor and play can borrow it from others and then share it with their spouses. It is important to try to maintain humor and play even in difficult times. It can be done. Viktor Frankl pointed out that humor helped people survive even in a Nazi concentration camp.[10] Humor "was another of the soul's weapons in the fight for self-preservation." More than anything else, he noted, humor can enable people to rise above any situation, even if only for a very few moments. Frankl said that he "practically trained" a fellow prisoner to develop a sense of humor by getting him to agree that they would each invent one funny story every day, a story based upon something that might happen after they were free again. Some people might naturally be, and some might have to teach their spouses how to be, humorous and playful. In either case, the marriage will benefit. In truth, a laugh a day may keep the dry-rot away.

FOOTNOTES

    1. Robert O. Blood, Jr. and Donald M. Wolfe, *Husbands and Wives: The Dynamics of Married Living* (Westport, Ct.: Greenwood Press, 1978), pp. 263–64.
    2. Zick Rubin, "Does Personality Really Change After 20?" *Psychology Today*, May, 1981, p. 27.
    3. Fyodor Dostoyevsky, *The Brothers Karamazov*, trans. Constance Garnett (New York: Signet, 1957), p. 324.
    4. Daniel Yankelovich, *New Rules: Searching for Self-Fulfillment in a World Turned Upside Down* (New York: Bantam Books, 1981), p. 239.

5. See Robert H. Lauer and Warren H. Handel, *Social Psychology: The Theory and Application of Symbolic Interactionism*, 2nd edition (Englewood Cliffs, N.J.: Prentice-Hall, 1983), p. 124 for a discussion.

6. See Robert H. Lauer, *Social Problems and the Quality of Life*, 3rd edition (Dubuque, Iowa: Wm. C. Brown, 1986), chapter 5.

7. Alfred North Whitehead, *Adventures of Ideas* (New York: Mentor Books, 1933), p. 273.

8. Mel Krantzler, *Creative Marriage* (New York: McGraw-Hill, 1981), p. 56.

9. R. William Betcher, "Intimate Play and Marital Adaptation," *Psychiatry* 44 (February, 1981):13–33.

10. Viktor E. Frankl, *Man's Search For Meaning* (Boston, Beacon Press, 1962), p. 42.

Chapter 9
What Is Most Important?

Someone has said that a baby cannot throw its toys out of its crib without influencing the farthest star. The saying reflects a perspective that has become well accepted—the interdependence of all things within a system. If one accepts the entire universe as a system, then anything that happens somewhere has repercussions throughout the system, however small those repercussions might be. If one accepts a family or a married couple as a system—and most social scientists do—then nothing in that system is unimportant to its functioning. In other words, the search for *a* key, *a* crucial variable in a long-term, satisfying marriage is fruitless. When you investigate something as complex as a changing, long-term relationship, there are seemingly hundreds of things that can make a difference. And because the relationship is a system, they all do make a difference.

Nevertheless, some things make more of a difference than others. All things are important, but not all are of equal importance. In this chapter, we will address the question of what things are most important. We will do this in a twofold way. First, we will discuss some things that are frequently believed to be important, but which are not, or at least are not for the majority of our couples. Second, we will report the things that our respondents said were most important in explaining their relationships.

THE BEST OF TIMES, THE WORST OF TIMES

Sarah, a midwestern statistician, has a 30-year marriage in which she is very happy. Looking back over it, she says that it has "included short-term boredom and frustration, anger and other negative feelings." She felt it was important to note this because she didn't want her relationship "to sound Pollyanna perfect." Her point is quite important. We have tried in various places to underscore it ourselves. Social scientists and marriage counselors and therapists stress it. Every marriage has its low as well as its high points. Even in a long-term, satisfying marriage, the spouses will likely experience both the best and the worst of times. The fairy-tale ending that "they lived happily ever after" is not only unrealistic but can be downright destructive if people believe it to be possible. Unfortunately, many people apparently believe that it is possible. They go into marriage with the idea that the relationship is a ticket to unabated and endless pleasure. They are deceived by the fairy tales and stories they have read into believing that the good marriage involves years of uninterrupted bliss. Such expectations inevitably crash into the frustrations of real life, sometimes leaving the individual so disillusioned that he or she opts for divorce as the only solution. A second or third marriage will prove to be no better, of course, as long as the expectations remain unchanged.

There are typical stresses in any long-term relationship, typical problems to be dealt with at the various stages of marriage.[1] One of the early crises, for instance, is the first serious conflict or the first recognition that one's spouse has certain habits that are irritating. There may be a disillusionment at that point, even a sense that the marriage may have been a terrible mistake. At succeeding stages of the relationship, if the marriage survives, there will be other typical crises. In addition, there are the atypical problems, those which are not necessarily a natural part of an evolving relationship, though they may occur with some frequency. For example, some couples have problems with in-laws. Others may have to deal with a serious drinking problem of a family member, or infidelity of one of the spouses, or a host of other events and problems that can intrude into the marriage. The question is, are our long-term, happily married couples satisfied with their relationships because they escaped such typical and atypical troubles? Are they the lucky few who have not been assaulted by the stresses and strains that afflict most couples?

We have already pointed out that our couples have had troubled times in their relationship. They are not happy because they have escaped either the minor annoyances or the major problems of life. We tried to get a clear picture of the checkered course of a satisfying marriage by asking our respondents to chart their satisfaction over time and to explain any high or low points. Figure 9.1 shows a few of the responses. There is no typical pattern in their satisfaction over time, no tendency for them to be alike in their experience of satisfaction. But they do clearly recognize the swings in their own marital experience. A few individuals drew either a straight line,

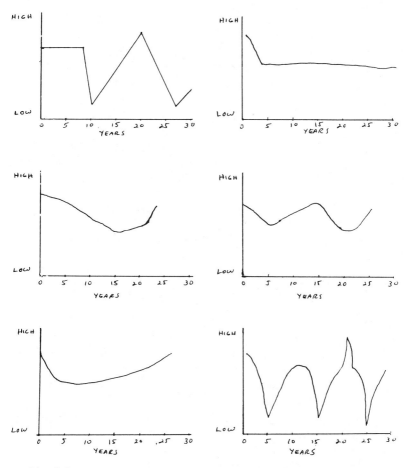

Fig. 9.1. Some of the charts of marital satisfaction drawn by the respondents.

indicating relatively the same level over the course of the marriage, or a rising, straight line, indicating a continually increasing sense of satisfaction. But the great majority portrayed variations in their satisfaction over time. For some, the variations were relatively small, while others recalled more pronounced swings. One wife, for instance, drew a straight line at a high point for most of her marriage. There was one dramatic dip, however. It was a time, she said, when she was dissatisfied with her marriage because she had gotten infatuated with another man. Her husband never knew about it. He remained patient and kind during the time, puzzled over his wife's dissatisfaction. Eventually, the phase passed.

Our respondents, in other words, have not had a fairy-tale existence. They have experienced the best of times and the worst of times. A husband said that his marriage was "healthy the first two years. The next ten were crazy, insane. The last three have been healing." Not many recalled such dramatic swings in their relationships, but nearly all talked about some low as well as some high years.

The high points sometimes referred to a particular event, such as the birth of a child, a new career, a period of financial well-being, and the empty nest experience. In some cases, the highs were a period when the couple, for whatever reasons, were functioning well together—they were truly a couple, sharing their experiences, their aspirations, their love.

What about low points? We shall look at them in a little more detail for two reasons. First, they emphasize the point that satisfying marriages may pass through some troubled years. Note that we said "years." Our respondents did not face problems that lasted only hours or days or even months; in some cases, they had to cope with years of difficulty. We discussed the meaning of commitment in terms of the willingness to endure difficult times and the determination to confront and work through problems. Those difficult times may last for some years (which is not to suggest, of course, that the spouses are miserable or experience no gratification during those times). Second, the kinds of things that make for low points are not idiosyncratic. Some problems are typical, not in the sense that they occur at a specific point in the marriage, but in the sense that many or even most couples will experience them. In particular, there are three broad types of problems that our couples mentioned as factors in low points—problems of adjustment, coping with crises, and dealing with children. Because the question of children is so complex, we will deal with it in a separate section below. Here we will look at the issues of adjustment and coping with crises.

Troubled as well as gratifying years may mark the course of a long-term, satisfying marriage.

Adjusting

Everyone knows that there is a period of adjustment early in a marriage. A newly-married woman told us: "You discover all sorts of little habits that you didn't know about and that annoy you."

Joan, a wife of 15 years, saw a somewhat different aspect of early adjustment:

> We were both well into our twenties when we married, thus quite set in our ways. The first few years, in retrospect, were not as satisfying due to our adjustment to giving instead of just taking.

Virtually everyone goes through a period of adjustment in the early years of marriage. What many people fail to realize (and therefore fail to expect) is that adjustment is likely to be demanded throughout a relationship. There will be adjustments at various points throughout the marriage, and these may involve a time of lowered satisfaction.

New roles are a common cause of the need for adjustment. It is unlikely that any couple today will escape the need to adjust to a new role on the part of a spouse. Becoming a parent, changing careers, and retiring all involve new roles. In addition, many couples face problems of adjustment because of the changing role of women. Gail is a technician who has been married for 27 years:

> When we were first married, I was very young and inexperienced. As time went by and our children started school, I was very bored and probably boring. I went to college and then to work, and this opened up a new world, so to speak. My husband and I had problems over this, because I saw and learned that there were a lot of other things besides housework and jumping to his demands. A few rough years and we were able to work that out. He is great now about helping with everything and the extra income helps us enjoy some things we wouldn't of otherwise had.

The low point of Gail's marriage, the "few rough years" of which she spoke, occurred between the tenth and fifteenth years.

Adjustment to a new or changing role may require not only a number of years but outside help. Mark is a minister who, in the thirtieth year of his marriage, just emerged from five years of difficulty:

> My wife has become more assertive over time and we had fairly severe difficulties from the 25th through the 29th years of our marriage. We went to a counselor who said we were

both stars. I think we need to be more aware of each other's achievements. I get greater satisfaction in all areas of my marriage when I enhance my mate rather than diminish her.

Mark's wife, like Gail, had gone back to school. She pursued a graduate degree while working full-time. She says she felt guilty about her decision, and had conflict with both her mother and her mother-in-law, neither of whom had sympathy with the roles of student and career woman that she had chosen. With the help of a counselor, however, they were emerging from the troubled years. Each had adjusted, and each believed that they were in a new phase of increasing satisfaction with their marriage.

Since change is inevitable in any long-term relationship, adjustment must be an ongoing process. Even when the change is of the type discussed in the last chapter, one spouse re-forming the other, adjustment will be necessary because the change efforts are rarely completely and quickly successful. And there may be times when there are unanticipated consequences when the change effort is successful. A husband may encourage his wife to be more self-reliant, and then face the unanticipated feeling of being unneeded by her. A woman may encourage her husband to improve his appearance, and then face the unanticipated feeling of jealousy when other women find him attractive. Or one spouse may encourage the other to pursue a career, only to find that the career makes more demands on time and energy than either had expected. Change is inevitable, and even when it is initiated it inevitably requires adjustment.

Adjustment is an ongoing process in any long-term marriage, a process of adapting to change in order to retain or restore a high level of satisfaction.

Coping with Crises

A second common reason for a low point in a marriage is a crisis of some sort—illness, unemployment, infidelity, death. A crisis does not always strain the relationship. In some cases, it can strengthen the bonds. When the spouses lean on each other for support, coping with a crisis enhances the marital relationship. But some crises, because of their length or severity, will strain even the best of marriages. Our couples were not immune from those stressful crises. Some of our respondents reported that physical or mental illness in the spouse marked a low point in their marital satisfaction. An extended or severe illness not only strains the time and energy of the healthy spouse, but also requires an adjustment to a different life style. A Texas wife told us that the one low point of her marriage occurred when her husband was quite ill with heart disease. He required continued care and she suddenly found herself confined to the home and engaged in nursing tasks. Moreover, there was the hovering question of his survival, which was a source of additional stress.

Mental disorders are also a source of stress. A Missouri husband identified his wife's period of deep depression as a low point in his marital satisfaction. "Professional help and medication and a change in our life style and living tempo has helped," he said. "High stress situations are generally avoided now. We are becoming more selective in our activities and generally consider each other and the family first."

Serious physical or mental illness may do more than place a temporary strain on a relationship. There can be a residue of disquiet or a dulling of the edge of satisfaction that lasts for many years. Corinne, a housewife, rates her marriage as "very happy." But she pointed out that the first low point in her 25-year marriage occurred after the first six years:

I had difficulty in dealing with his periods of depression. I saw to it that we spent a lot of time with a couple around whom he seemed to feel less depressed. Then I became jealous of the wife, because she seemed to have such a good rapport with my husband. There was no sexual basis for this jealousy, and I did not suspect that there was. We seldom see the couple any more. But the jealousy has been a bother to me in varying degrees ever since. We got counseling and that has helped me minimize this. But I still don't want to see her anymore.

Generally, Corinne is highly satisfied with her relationship with her husband, but the struggle with her husband's depression and her own feelings about the woman who seemed to lift his spirits has left an emotional scar.

Corinne affirms her husband's fidelity with confidence, though the observer cannot help but see a small shadow of doubt cast over her words. Her case raises the question of the extent to which those in long-term, satisfying marriages have to deal with the matter of infidelity. It is difficult to know how many Americans engage in extramarital affairs. A number of polls have been taken by various magazines and the results vary considerably.[2] Sixty-five percent of women in a *Playboy* poll, but only 21 percent in a *Ladies' Home Journal* poll, admitted to being sexually unfaithful to their spouses. Such results are not surprising in view of the diverse readers of the two magazines. The actual figure undoubtedly lies somewhere between the two results. According to a *Psychology Today* poll, between one-third and one-half of married people have affairs.

In spite of the figures, most Americans disapprove of extramarital sex.[3] We did not ask our respondents about fidelity directly, but we are inclined to believe that it is not a major problem with them. They appear to take their commitment seriously, and part of the meaning of commitment is fidelity to the other and mutual trust. Infidelity is incongruous with all of the qualities of friendship, agape love, and commitment stressed by our subjects. At the same time, we all have incongruities in our lives. We would be surprised if there were no cases of infidelity and no suspicion of infidelity. The point is not that our respondents totally escaped the crisis of infidelity, but that by the very nature of their relationship they were less likely than others to have to deal with it.

Only two of those we questioned volunteered that they had had brief affairs. A few others had to deal with the suspicion of infidelity or with jealousy. As one husband, happy in his 25-year marriage, told us, the low point in his relationship had occurred just four years previously when "there was a question of fidelity and the possibility of divorce." As it turned out, there was no infidelity and there was no divorce. Some claimed that infidelity would be the one problem that would be difficult for them to accept. A wife of 27 years said that although she could work out almost any problem with her husband given enough time, infidelity "would probably not be something I could forget and forgive."

Nevertheless, marriages can, and frequently do, survive infidelity. The acid test is not what one thinks one would do in prospect, but what one would actually do if the situation arose. We do not doubt that most of our respondents could deal with this problem as they have dealt with every other kind of problem.

Yet another kind of crisis is unemployment, which is a traumatic experience for most people. Unemployment is associated with higher rates of suicide, mental illness, physical ailments, and psychosomatic symptoms.[4] Fatal heart attacks and strokes among men over the age of 45 peak about a year after unemployment rates reach their highest level. After the loss of a job, the worker is likely to experience depression, anxiety, aggression, insomnia, the loss of self-esteem, and marital problems. The spouse of the unemployed worker tends to develop psychiatric symptoms. Unemployment adversely affects both the individual and the individual's relationships.

A number of our respondents discussed the ways in which periods of unemployment stressed their marriages. A husband who is now "very happy" in his 29-year marriage identified a low point between the 21st and 25th years. At that time, unemployment "caused stress on me. Communication failed. For a year or two, it affected our feelings for one another." His wife described her feelings during and after those troubled years:

> My husband went through an extended period of unemployment when we had been married for 22 or 23 years. It seemed he was not interested in working, was satisfied to draw unemployment benefits and let me carry the load. We had two children in college and the last one was a senior in high school. I thought he had forgotten our goals. He did not care about our partnership, I thought. Because he does not share his feelings much, I did not know his own views much. I did not know his views of the situation until I began praying for him daily. His weaknesses and fears were made known to me. I forgave him everything. When my attitude changed, so did his.

Now, she says, they enjoy each other more than ever. They learned to work together to meet the problem of his unemployment. Her husband has been unemployed a few times since, but it has not been as traumatic because they learned how to handle it as a team. She realized that he was not indifferent to the problem and he realized that she needed to know how he felt about the problem. They learned to approach subsequent periods of unemployment as a problem-solving time rather than a fault-finding time. The result is a stronger and more satisfying relationship for both of them.

Crises may depress marital satisfaction in the short run, but when managed as a mutual problem-solving situation they can enhance satisfaction and strengthen the relationship in the long run.

THE ROLE OF CHILDREN

For those in mixed or unhappy marriages, as we noted earlier, children are a very important factor in holding the marriage together. What about in the happy marriages? In response to the open-ended question about "anything else that is important in your marriage," about 14 percent of the respondents chose to talk about their children or grandchildren. Their comments are interesting in light of the findings by other researchers on the relationships between marital satisfaction and presence of children. In general, the evidence suggests that marital satisfaction declines during the child-rearing years and tends to increase once the children have left home.[5] Does this mean that children, who are desired by most married couples, are more of a burden than the blessing they were expected to be? The answer is sometimes they are and sometimes they are not. But in any case, the children, like marriage itself, are likely to involve both the worst of times and the best of times in a long-term, satisfying relationship. Sir Francis Bacon wrote about the paradox of children when he pointed out that they increase the cares of life, but mitigate the remembrance of death. Among our couples, children increased the cares of life, but they also increased the satisfaction. Let us look first at the down side of the paradox, the increased cares.

Children as a Burden

Some of the burdens of child-rearing, according to our couples, are the drain on time and energy and the fact that children can be a source of stress and conflict. There is a tendency for the children to divert attention away from the marital relationship, for spouses to neglect each other and their relationship in the course of attending to all of the needs of the children. Researchers have found, for example, that women with children are less likely than those without children to engage in outside activities with their spouses, exchange stimulating ideas with their spouses, work on a project together, or calmly engage in a discussion of some sort.[6]

Mary Anne is a flight attendant who has been married for 15 years. She drew a chart of marital satisfaction that showed a leveling off when her children were born:

> Having two children after 10 years of marriage has had its advantages and disadvantages. It has been an adjustment to say

the least. We have others to consider and don't spend as much time together as I would like for us to. I think my husband has changed a great deal in that he is not as considerate as he was when we were first married. This disturbs me, but I can only hope that he will come to realize that I still need a little special attention now and then.

Other respondents noted similar problems of too little attention to each other, too little time to cultivate the marital relationship, during the child-bearing years.

The burden of children is more, of course, than simply a drain on time and energy. There are, as one wife put it, the "trials and tribulations of raising children." Some of our couples reported conflict with each other as a result of the strains over, and sometimes disagreement about, raising children:

> The methods used to raise the children were perhaps the area of least mutual agreement and became the greatest source of continuing conflict. Our thought processes grew relatively close together except in the area of how to instill the desired values in our children. We wanted the same result but didn't agree on the path to that result and that constantly caused conflict and threat to the marriage. The underlying knowledge that we both wanted the same result probably kept the conflict from exploding into irreconcilable differences.

Even if a couple agree and try to support each other, the stress involved in raising a child can strain the marital bonds. Sometimes a problem may appear more severe at the time than it does in retrospect. A seemingly incorrigible child may grow up to be a source of enormous gratification to the parents. Present stress in child-rearing does not mean ultimate disillusionment. At the same time, that present stress colors every aspect of a parent's life, as a California housewife illustrates:

> One factor that is going on in my marriage is that we—and especially me—are having a lot of difficulty with our 16-year-old daughter. She's just miserable to have in the house. My unhappiness and frustration with her are probably coloring how I respond to this questionnaire in that she's got me very upset with life. Walt is very supportive of me and we're

working together to deal with this problem. I don't know what I would do if I were alone to deal with this problem.

The problem may not be an incorrigible or rebellious child. It may be a case of agonizing over problems that the child has, academic problems, problems with friends, or problems of health. A handicapped child may add considerable stress to the marital relationship. A child with a serious illness of some sort may test a marriage to the breaking point. Ralph and Evelyn have a 17-year marriage that both regard as highly satisfying. But they came near to breaking apart because of the illness of their daughter. Listen first to Evelyn:

> The level of satisfaction went up after the first uncertain year of marriage when we were trying to understand our own and each other's roles. The graph then descends at about two to three years when we came to the realization that our daughter was ill and would be ill for some years, until she grew out of it—if she didn't die first, of course. The level of satisfaction then begins to climb as we learned to live with our daughter's illness and it has continued to climb as we realized our daughter has outgrown her illness.

Evelyn didn't mention it, but a good part of the problem was Ralph's attitude, as he admits:

> I had a high when we were first married, because I couldn't see that there were some problems. I thought all was perfect, but my wife didn't. With the birth of our daughter, who was seriously ill for the first seven years, I had a low. During the low, I became a verbal child abuser. My wife says that I was a good father more than I was a bad one, but she did mention divorce if I didn't get myself together. She tried to help me see my problem. I did see it but couldn't control my mouth.

Finally, Ralph did learn to control his mouth as a result of a religious experience. He and Evelyn agree that their marriage is now stronger and more gratifying than it was in the past.

Overall, those of our respondents who had reached the empty nest or adult children stage tended to agree with the pattern reported above—marital satisfaction increases once the difficult child-rearing years are past. This is not to say that the child-rearing years are unhappy ones. As one husband said, the children "added to and took away from our happiness at different times." What would be the net result of that adding to and taking away? To answer the question, let us look at the other side of the coin, the blessing of children.

In long-term marriages, satisfaction tends to be depressed during the child-rearing years.

The Blessings of Children

In spite of the depressed satisfaction with the marriage during the child-rearing years, our respondents indicated that their children enriched their lives and enhanced their marital solidarity. Couples of all ages—from those married 15 years to those who have been together 50 years—spontaneously mentioned their children as an important factor in the success of their marriage. Some recalled the birth of a child as a high point in their lives. Others talked about their involvement in their children's activities being a meaningful part of their lives. Thus, they are aware of the paradox of children. They speak about the blessings and, at the same time, they also recognize that the children added strains and concerns. As one wife summed it up: "Children are a treasure, burden, and responsibility all in one, but they are most important."

For the most part, happily-married couples believe that their children are a cohesive force in their marriage. For many of them, one of the purposes in marriage is to have a family. Their children are one of the reasons that they want their marriage to work. The children, said a husband, are "the glue that stuck us together." Again, we encounter the paradox however. For children can strain as well as enhance solidarity. Gary pointed out that the "lowest point" in his 25-year marriage was "when the children were small and the money was tight." Indeed, there is some evidence from a national survey that marital satisfaction is low when the children are very young.[7] At that point, the demands on the time and energy of the parents are great. A child entering the home creates an entirely different world for the parents. "Marriage was an adjustment," noted Bill, a manager, "but nothing changes your life as drastically as having a child." Another husband pointed out that the children had prevented him and his wife from doing many things "since we have put them first so often."

As the children get older, however, the demands may diminish. The couple may find that their relationship with each other improves, that they are entering a new era of companionship with the bonds of their marital relationship intensified by their shared experiences of parenthood. Gary pointed out that, while his marriage was least satisfactory when the children were small, as the children "grew older they seemed to pull us together." A wife of 30 years said that she and her husband had grown closer together "particularly with our children older—still close—but not demanding our constant attention." A Southern California woman, "very happy" in her 39-year marriage, summed up the kind of experience we are discussing here:

> As our marriage matured, we became closer emotionally and physically. The children played a big part in our closeness. It helped to know that we did a good job in raising them.

For many couples, then, children provide a significant part of the purpose and meaning of marriage, even though they recognize that the children add strains. The children give the couple a focus outside of themselves. The children become a joint project in which husband and wife take pride of a shared achievement. There is always a danger, of course, of slipping over the precarious line between an outside focus that enhances a relationship and an absorption that neglects the relationship. Those in enduring and satisfying marriages tend to stay on the safe side of the line. They take pride in their children. They find an added dimension of love in their lives because of their children. But they also recognize that their own relationship was prior to that of their children and will continue when the children are no longer around.

We discussed earlier the fact that couples with long-term, unhappy marriages gave the children as a primary reason for staying together. Children can be a cohesive factor even when they are a strain on the marital relationship. They can be the fragile bond that holds a deteriorating relationship together. They can also be the focus of a joint project that enhances as well as solidifies a relationship. The difference hinges upon the extent to which a couple recognizes the importance of their relationship and the necessity of continual work on their relationship. Marvin and Judy have been married for 15 years. They have two children, and both rate their marriage as a happy one. But they have a potential for problems in the future, for Marvin told us: "Our life together as husband and wife was never as rich as it is as father and mother."

The parent who depends upon the children for gratification, who is happy with the marriage primarily because of the children, is imposing on the children a responsibility which they cannot and will not continue to bear. Children are not the solution to a flawed relationship. But they may add a new dimension of richness to a good relationship.

Children may enhance the satisfaction and solidarity of a marriage when a couple recognizes that they must continue to build their own relationship as well as engage in the task of parenting.

THE ROLE OF RELIGION

In chapter 1, we noted that religion is not the critical factor in an enduring marriage. The religious composition of our sample was very close to the religious composition of the American public. We need to balance that statement here by pointing out that a number of couples specifically mentioned their religious faith as an important ingredient in their marriages. Less than 5 percent of the respondents identified religious faith as important, but those who did believed that it is the foundation of a happy marriage. Susan, a homemaker and part-time piano teacher, said:

I think that religious commitment is the most important ingredient in our marriage. While my husband's level of interest in spiritual matters is not as deep as mine, we are both very active in our local church and are both very conscious of Christian principles. Even before I made my commitment to God, I was keenly aware that I had promised before Him to love, honor, and cherish my husband.

Another wife said that she and her husband "strongly believe in praying together daily and having Christ as the center of our home and marriage. He has blessed us abundantly."

What is it that religion does for people? For some, it is the basis for commitment. Their religious faith does not allow them to consider divorce as an option. Jim, happily married for 41 years, said that religion was one of the most important reasons for the stability of his marriage:

> All our children went to Catholic school and so did we as children. We come from large Catholic families. We did not believe in birth control or divorce. We had strong rules and people lived by them. We never expected anything else.

A wife of 17 years, also Catholic, similarly stressed the importance of the Church's teaching:

> We know the Church does not encourage divorce. Probably as a result, we did a lot of thinking and discussing before we were married to be sure we had the makings for a lasting marriage.

The religious beliefs of the happy couples do more than solidify their commitment, however. They are not like the unhappy couple that we discussed earlier who grimly hang on to a relationship that leaves them miserable because their religion forbids them to do anything else. The happy couples find their religious faith to be a source of nourishment as well as stability in the marriage. Kevin is a claims manager who has been married 21 years:

> I think a strong and healthy relationship with God that is shared by the mate is vital. It has helped me in feeling and believing that God somehow directed our lives together and daily supports and sustains our marriage. Marriage is a journey into life with a special person as a companion. The challenge is to grow together and avoid consciously that which weakens this goal.

Others mentioned the fact that their religious beliefs are the basis for their decision-making process, for dealing with problems of various kinds, and for strength and guidance in the face of crisis. As a Georgia husband of 15 years put it:

> We have many problems in life but we have always helped each other through the power of God's words and we have come through many storms to much clearer skies. From being tossed to and fro, we now have positive attitudes because of many scriptures in the Bible that we use. Somehow those scriptures are what give us strength and we say this by experience and not just lip service.

For some people, then, religion is seen as an important part of their marital relationship. To return to our systems perspective, this does not mean that it is unimportant to the rest, but only that they regard other things as more important in explaining the stability of and satisfaction with their marriage.

Religious beliefs and practices are an important foundation for the marital stability and satisfaction of some people, but most regard other factors as of greater importance.

THE MOST IMPORTANT INGREDIENTS

We want to stress the fact that in answering the question of what is most important, we are giving the responses of our respondents to a specific question. That is, we asked them to select from 39 factors those most important in explaining their marriage. We then asked them to identify anything else that was important which are neither listed among the 39 factors nor salient to the respondents. For instance, we pointed out that good conflict management skills are very important, and that our couples have and use those skills.

On the other hand, it is necessary to understand the situation from the point of view of the respondents. These are couples who have achieved what virtually all American couples envision when they pledge themselves to each other in marriage. How do they explain their success? What factors do they regard as most important in their own experience? Following are the reasons given by husbands and wives, listed in order of frequency named:

MEN	WOMEN
My spouse is my best friend.	My spouse is my best friend.
I like my spouse as a person.	I like my spouse as a person.
Marriage is a long-term commitment.	Marriage is a long-term commitment.
Marriage is sacred.	Marriage is sacred.
We agree on aims and goals.	We agree on aims and goals.
My spouse has grown more interesting.	My spouse has grown more interesting.

I want the relationship to succeed.

An enduring marriage is important to social stability.

We laugh together.

I am proud of my spouse's achievements.

We agree on a philosophy of life.

We agree about our sex life.

We agree on how and how often to show affection.

I confide in my spouse.

We share outside hobbies and interests.

I want the relationship to succeed.

We laugh together.

We agree on a philosophy of life.

We agree on how and how often to show affection.

An enduring marriage is important to social stability.

We have a stimulating exchange of ideas.

We discuss things calmly.

We agree about our sex life.

I am proud of my spouse's achievements.

As may be seen, the first seven reasons most frequently named were exactly the same for the men and the women, even though they responded individually and independently! Overall, there was a rank-order correlation of over .90 between the husbands' and the wives' lists. This was a surprising finding. We did not expect such consensus to emerge. The fact that it did underscores the importance of the factors identified.

Both men and women are saying the same thing about the most important reason for their long-term, satisfying marriage. In essence: "I am involved in an intimate relationship with someone I like and enjoy being with." As one wife summed it up, "I feel that liking a person in marriage is as important as loving that person. Friends enjoy each other's company. We spend an unusually large amount of time together." It isn't that sex or passion are unimportant; it is simply that other things are more important. Without the sense of friendship, the enjoyment of being with the other and sharing in various activities, sex or passion or romantic feelings are powerless to weld a long-term, meaningful union. Our happy couples have a shared history that is gratifying to them and they look forward to a shared future. As a wife, reflecting on her marriage, told us: "I really hope we grow old together."

It may seem almost trite to say that "my spouse is my best friend," but as many counselors and therapists know, there are a lot of people who are married to each other who do not feel that way. One marriage therapist with whom we shared the results said to us:

> I agree. It is consistent with my own experience, both as a therapist and as a husband. Fran and I cherish our friendship. We have a good marriage because we really like each other and we like being together and doing things together.

Or as one of the wives in our sample said of her husband, "I would want to have him as a friend even if I weren't married to him." Our respondents not only like each other and cherish each other as friends, but tend to find each other becoming more interesting over time. A man married for 30 years said that it was almost like being married to a series of different women:

> I have watched her grow and have shared with her both the pain and the exhilaration of her journey. I find her more fascinating now than when we were first married.

As noted earlier, a common theme among the couples was that the things they really liked in each other were qualities of caring, giving, integrity, and a sense of humor.

The second key to a lasting marriage is a belief in marriage as a long-term commitment and a sacred institution. Many of our respondents thought that the present generation takes the vow "till death do us part" too lightly, that young people today are unwilling to work through difficult times. As Bill, a college administrator married for over 20 years, said:

> Commitment means a willingness to be unhappy for awhile. I wouldn't go on for years and years being wretched in my marriage. But you can't avoid troubled times. You're not going to be happy with each other all the time. That's when commitment is really important.

Our respondents want their relationship to succeed and are willing to work hard to make it succeed. They are committed to each other for better and for worse, and they know that their shared histories will have some of each.

A third key, undoubtedly important to both the friendship and the commitment, is consensus. Our respondents perceive agreement between themselves about aims and goals and their philosophy of life. As many social psychological studies show, we tend to like people who are like us. Similarity is an important basis for friendship. Similar aims and goals facilitate friendship, including the friendship of those who are married. They also make it somewhat easier to maintain commitment. Most people encounter enough problems and frustrations in life without the added burden of battling a spouse over fundamental aims and goals.

A fourth key is humor. Laugher is medicine for the human spirit. Laughing together increases intimacy and adds luster to the shared history of a couple.

While all of the above factors would be rated as important by therapists, there were some beliefs and practices among our couples that contradict what at least some therapists believe is important to a marriage. We have largely noted these in previous chapters, but will briefly review them here. One is the manner of handling conflict. Our couples stressed the importance of *not* "letting it all hang out" in conflict. They insisted that spouses should not freely vent their anger with each other, but should wait until they can engage in a relatively calm discussion about a problem. A second commonly held belief that contradicts the conventional wisdom concerns equality in marriage. The notion that marriage is a "50-50" proposition can be damaging, according to our couples. In the long run, the giving and taking in a marriage should balance out. But if either partner enters a marriage determined that all transactions must be equal, the relationship will suffer.

Third, some marriage experts advocate that spouses maintain separate as well as shared interests. Our respondents point out that they try to maximize their time together. They agree that it is important to maintain individual identities, to have some individual interests and pursuits, but they suggest that the most likely danger is a failure to become a couple rather than a merging of identities. During the working years, a certain amount of individuality is built into the lives of a couple by virtue of separate worlds of work experience. The need then is to focus on being a couple, on continuing to build the marital relationship. We did not detect any loss of individuality as a result of this emphasis. Couples did not agree and did not even perceive agreement on all matters. Their intense intimacy, their preference for shared rather than separate activities, seems to reflect a richness and fulfillment in the relationship rather than a loss of identity. As one husband pointed out:

On occasion she has something else to do, and I enjoy the time alone. But it strikes me that I can enjoy it because I know that soon she will be home, and we will be together again.

Finally, marriage experts have pointed out the corrosion of time, the tendency for satisfaction to inevitably decline. The overall impression we get from reading the literature and talking to counselors and therapists is that only a tiny fraction at best of all couples can hope to achieve a union that is both long-lasting and deeply satisfying. That may or may not be true empirically, but we do not believe that it is inherently true. Tolstoy was not right in saying that happy families are all alike, but neither, we believe, is it correct to say that there are no common factors in happy unions. It is true that there is "no single thread," no single quality that distinguishes the healthy from the unhealthy family.[8] But there is a combination of factors, those which we have identified in this book, that can be used by couples to achieve what the 300 couples who responded to our survey achieved. The point is that couples are not inherently doomed to either divorce or the slow, corrosive decline into a dull or bland relationship. There will be high points and low points, but those who persevere and work at it can be amply rewarded with a continual recapturing of the intense satisfactions of the early days of the relationship. As an engineer, married 28 years, told us:

> The nature of our interaction has been one of mutual caring, with the change over time akin to a sine wave which peaked positively after the first ten years, then dipped negatively during the next ten, with the curve heading upward these last eight years. I guess the main reason we remained together so long is that we are really good friends. We have not had the pleasure of being alone with each other for any length of time until recently. So we are kind of like newlyweds, without responsibilities for anyone other than ourselves for the first time in many years. Feels a little strange, but neat.

People explain their long-term, satisfying marriages mainly in terms of four keys: having a spouse who is one's best friend and whom one likes as a person; commitment to marriage and to the spouse; consensus on fundamentals; and shared humor.

ACTION GUIDELINES

All of the action guidelines of the previous chapters could be brought together here, for in this chapter we have rank ordered topics covered in previous chapters. The ordering identifies the relative importance of those previous chapters. Thus, our action guidelines for this chapter stress the importance of going back to chapter 5 to review the guidelines involved in liking one's mates and to chapter 4 to review the guidelines about commitment. In addition, however, this chapter has underscored the importance of expectations about marriage.

Although most couples pledge themselves to each other for better or for worse, they make the unrealistic assumption that for them the times are mainly, if not always, going to be better. Furthermore, many Americans take seriously the notion that they have a God-given right to happiness, and that any threat to their unhappiness should be eliminated. The first experience of unhappiness in a relationship, therefore, may be quite painful. Since the unhappy times are inevitable, it is healthier to acknowledge at the outset that those times must be accepted, confronted, and worked through *as a couple.* Chapter 7 provides guidelines for working through those times that involve differences or conflict between the couple. In addition, it can help if a spouse reminds himself or herself during troubled times that this is one of those inevitable low points of marriage but that, working together, the two of them will get through it. In essence, a healthy approach would be to expect troubles, expect to work through those troubles, and expect the marriage to be stronger and more satisfying as a result.

FOOTNOTES

1. Sander J. Breiner, "Sequential Chronological Stress in the Family," *Family Therapy* 7 (no. 8, 1980):247–54.

2. The statistics in this paragraph are cited in Robert H. Lauer, *Social Problems and the Quality of Life,* 3rd edition (Dubuque, Iowa: Wm. C. Brown, 1986), chapter 3.

3. Carol Tavris, "Masculinity," *Psychology Today,* January, 1977, pp. 35–42; *Public Opinion,* October/November, 1982, p. 34.

4. See Robert H. Lauer, *op. cit.,* chapter 9.

5. Boyd C. Rollins and Harold Feldman, "Marital Satisfaction Over the Family Life Cycle," in R. Winch and G. B. Spanier, eds., *Selected Studies in Marriage and the Family* (New York: Holt, Rinehart & Winston, 1974), pp. 422–23.

6. S. A. Anderson, C. S. Russell and W. Schumm, "Perceived Marital Quality and

Family Life-cycle Categories: A Further Analysis,'' *Journal of Marriage and the Family* 45 (February: 1983):127–39.

7. Norval D. Glenn and Charles N. Weaver, ''A Multivariate, Multisurvey of Marital Happiness,'' *Journal of Marriage and the Family* 40 (May, 1978):269–78.

8. Jerry M. Lewis, W. Robert Beavers, John T. Gossett, and Virginia Austin Phillips, *No Single Thread* (New York: Brunner/Mazel, 1976).

Index

A

Abortion 18
Acceptance, of spouse 57,85,
 141–143
Accommodation, in conflict 120,129,
 132,133
Action guidelines 184
 for change 157–160
 for commitment 62–65
 for communication 107–109
 for conflict 132–135
 for concensus 109
 for love 84–88
 for togetherness 109–110
Activities
 individual 102–103,104
 shared 37,98–99,104–106,180,
 182–183
Adjustment 166–168
 Dyadic Scale of 13n.
Affection
 as component of love 68,74–76
 expression of 74–76,86,148
 marital satisfaction and 147–148
Aggression, expression of 127–128,
 130
Agreement
 in consensus patterns 96–100
 in sexual relations 70–71,72,99
Aims, marital satisfaction and 146–147,
 149,179,182
Apartness, see also Individuality,
 maintenance of
 togetherness versus 103–106
Attitudes, changes of 151–153
Avoidance, of conflict 118,120

B

Behavior
 feelings and 84–85
 interpretation of 123–124

C

Caring 80,82,86
Change, marital satisfaction and
 138–145
 action guidelines for 157–160
 in deepening of affection 147–148
 in interpersonal skills 147
 in life aims and goals 146–147
 management of 148–150
 through mutual education
 150–155,158–160
 in personality 141–143
 in role changes 143–145
Child abuse
 incidence 17
 in single-parent families 40
Children
 agreement regarding 99
 continuance of marriage for 37,
 39–40,41
 effects of divorce on 16–17,53
 illegitimate 18
 illness of 174
 remarriage and 45,46
 role of 172–177
 of single-parents 40
 as source of conflict 114,115–116
 as source of marital enrichment
 175–177
 as source of stress 172–175
 in stepfamilies 40
 unwanted 18
Cognitive dissonance 85
Cohabitation
 incidence 9,18
 marriage and 9–11
 differences between 10
 second marriage and 10–11
Collaboration, in conflict 120,132–133
Commitment, marital 37,42,47–65
 acceptance of spouse and 57
 action guidelines for 62–65